Re

Without Rules

by Keith Beasley

A guide to freedom - for all those with an interest in personal self development, spirituality, awareness, enlightenment and in Reiki - or any other form of healing.

Dedicated to my students . . . for teaching me so much

Published by Lulu: www.lulu.com

Categories: Mind Body & Spirit, Self Help, Spirituality, Meditation, Healing, New Age

ISBN 978-1-84799-866-8

Cover illustration: *Japanese Garden* by Liz Allen

Reiki - Without Rules

Foreword

From virtually unknown in the 1980's Reiki Healing has rapidly entered mainstream society with regular features on TV, the Internet, Radio and in magazines world-wide. But what *is* it? Each author on the subject adds their own rules, each practitioner does it slightly differently, each Master teaches their own brand. Which is the true Reiki?

All of them! The beauty of Reiki *is* that it is 'all things to all men'. The joy of Reiki *is* its simplicity. The truth of Reiki is for each of us to determine in our own way in our own time.

In this book, Keith Beasley, Reiki Master and teacher, puts Reiki and its variants into perspective. He shows how Reiki works best when allowed to do what it has to. Reiki is beyond beliefs and follows no rules. Through Reiki we can each learn to be our true selves, to live in Reiki and let Reiki live in us.

Ah, so Reiki is 'the light'? Yes, it is the light of enlightenment, the Chi of Tai-Chi, the Qi of Qi-gong, the Prana of yoga and the love of God.

Whatever your background, whatever your chosen path, Reiki has something to offer you . . . but you might well call it by another name. And that doesn't matter. In fact, nothing really matters! As we become aware of our spiritual nature and allow our inner/higher self to live in us and through us, then life takes on a new, real, meaning. Reiki, as a method of healing, assists in this process. In can transform this process. Together with all the many other wonderful therapies and holistic approaches to life we now have, it can transform our society and/or our minds . . . for are they not the same thing?

About the Author

Keith Beasley is self-employed as a Reiki Master/Teacher. He lives Reiki. He IS Reiki . . . as are we all! He says, of his experience of Reiki: "it has helped me to reunite my mind/body with my soul. To reconnect to my true, inner, higher, self. To BE the real me."

Prior to Reiki (which he 'learnt' in 1995/6) he had for some years been exploring various philosophies, religions and techniques - from Dowsing in 1987, through Yoga, Alexander Technique, etc. These gradually opened him up from his factual scientific upbringing. Reiki 'arrived' as his job in Quality Assurance in the electronics industry had ceased to be fulfilling. It was time for a 'leap of faith'.

As he began to teach Reiki (from 1996) so it's power and truth left their mark - or rather, the now outdated, unreal, thoughts and beliefs began to fall by the wayside. In Reiki, and in life itself, he found a whole new world opening up - or rather, being reawakened. Through sharing experiences and ideas with students and other Masters, so the deeper significance of Reiki began to shine though. Reiki IS love, it is light. WE are love, We are light.

Fine in theory, but what does that mean in practice? As the years move on so the world of love, light and spirit become not just principles but, increasingly, reality. Life itself is our teacher. Reiki and it's teachers, like Masters in other areas of life, are merely enablers on the path.

In 2002 Keith met artist Liz Allen and moved from Northamptonshire where he'd been born and brought up. For two years they lived near Brighton developing Pintados Healing Art: their unique combination of healing, art, divination and empathic consultations . . . for both their own benefit and growth . . . and as a business.

In 2005 they moved to the mountains of the Monchique in the Western Algarve where they run retreats embracing their workshops and approach to spiritual development: see www.pintados.co.uk

Reiki - Without Rules

Contents

Illustrations and Diagrams

Reiki - Without Rules

Visualisations & Exercises

Reiki - Without Rules

WHAT IS REIKI?

1 - The Energy

"Reiki", the "Life Force Energy" is the vital life force that is within and around all things. It is the energy that turns caterpillars into butterflies and that makes every snowflake different. It is life itself.

This is easy to say, but not so easy to fully appreciate. So we'll start with the word "Reiki" - a Japanese word and thus virtually impossible to translate accurately. The Japanese character, or kanji, can be interpreted in many different ways. That is the nature of Japanese and other symbol based languages: these have a sense and feeling rather than a literal, linguistic meaning.

So what is the *sense* of the word? *Universal* - that which transcends. It also has a rather mystical, magical quality - transcendence not just in the physical sense, but beyond explanation, or even description.

We can equate Reiki to 'the life force' that is accessed in other Eastern practices: the Chi of Tai Chi, the Prana of Yoga and the Qi of Qi Gong. They are the same thing. The energy of life itself.

In Western, or at least Christian terms, Reiki is God . . . or at least God's healing energy . . . depending on your definitions.

At the more day-to-day level, Reiki is Love. Universal, Unconditional, Love that is, not the limited human love that is often meant by the term.

Reiki is also 'Light' - as in the idea of Enlightenment and 'seeing the light'. Whether you call it Light, Love or Reiki, it is a vibrational energy . . . and omnipotent. Nothing can stand in its way . . . and yet it is also nurturing, supportive, gentle, calming. It is all things to all men.

Reiki - Without Rules

Nature's Blue-print

Every snow-flake is unique

**Since when did nature ever
do anything the same twice?**

There are No Rules!

Another key feature of Reiki, the Energy, is that it is omniscient - it senses all, knows all. There is no escaping from it. This can be a scary thought, until we learn to appreciate that Reiki is within us and part of us. Not some separate, dictatorial God, but the 'God within'; always with our best interests at heart (although sometimes we might doubt it!). Reiki is thus that part of us that lies deep within - our inner or higher self, our soul, our essence.

Because Reiki *is* all things and knows all things (by being part of them) it is also the ultimate wisdom. Only a fool argues with it . . .

Reiki - Without Rules

unfortunately most of us are still fools.

There is nothing new in all of this. What I describe as Reiki, other religions and philosophies through the ages have known about and helped us access in their own ways. Often this message has been lost and/or overshadowed by ritual and religious fervour, but look deep enough into the origins of most (if not all) religions and philosophies and the concept of a Universal Creative Force is there. That is all that Reiki is.

From words to experience

But Reiki is far more than a word. It cannot be defined. It has to be *experienced*. If a picture paints a thousand words, then an experience paints a thousand pictures . . . and an experience thus paints a million words. There is no alternative to actually trying something ourselves. No matter how many books we read, videos or TV programmes we watch we can rarely enter into the true spirit of something without first hand experience. Included in this book are thus a number of visualisations and other exercises which you're encouraged to have a go at. Some might not work for you, but don't worry! Don't be afraid to change the details to suit your own interests. Reiki *is* experiential. The intent of this book is not just to inform but to inspire and to enable true Reiki experiences.

In Love

When in a Reiki (healing) experience we are, quite literally, 'in love'. Our whole mind, body and soul is immersed in divine love and light. With practice this sensation can be extended from a healing treatment session into our day to day life. Thus we can begin to live 'in the light' or 'in love'.

The conventional human notion of being 'in love' by contrast is often a different sensation:

IN LOVE

ROMANTICALLY	DIVINELY
Can't sleep, eat or focus on anything properly	Totally aware of all that's going on around
Single focus of attention	Able to focus on whatever is important in the here and now
Often short lived	A way of life, eternal
When it ends, leaves us devastated	If it ends, leaves us calm, happy and peaceful

From this we see that romantic love is often a poor substitute for the real thing. Unfortunately we've been brought up to the notion that romantic love, love for a single special partner, is the 'be all and end all'. This, we're lead to believe, is true love. Sometimes it is. Sometimes a romance *is* 'made in heaven' and is part of a life of divine living, but how often? Through Reiki we begin to explore divine love and can see romantic love for what it is. When it *is* based on a higher truth, we'll be able to embrace it with mind, body and soul. When it isn't, the Reiki will help us to see the realities, and not get so upset by its ending or limitations. For me, and I suspect for many, practising Reiki gives soppy romantics an opportunity to 'grow up', to put our lovey dovey images into perspective.

Aspects of Love

If failed relationships seem to dog you and leave you oscillating between emotional highs and lows, then you'll hopefully find that the broader, deeper, sense of love that comes through Reiki will be of great help. This is why I took to Reiki. With its help I've been able to see and experience other aspects of love, and thus put romantic love into a realistic perspective. It's important, often a necessary form of love . . . but by no means the only one:

Reiki can be seen as 'Community Spirit' and 'Lord of the Dance', it is that which is behind the wider manifestations of love in the world. All love is God's love. It's Universal, everywhere, expressed in innumerable ways. We just tend to give it different names depending on who or what we're loving. By looking at the following Aspects of Love, we can expand this idea:

Aspects of Love

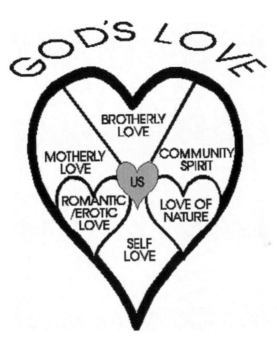

To feel whole we need to experience love in all aspects of our lives.

Reiki exists and can be applied to all aspects of love.

Love changes everything

Motherly Love

Of all forms of human love, motherly love perhaps approaches divine love most closely, in that it is unconditional. It is a love given without any expectation of anything in return. It is a caring love, a dependency - *but only where that dependency is born of necessity.* This proviso is an important one. Motherly love applies where the object of that love isn't *capable* of returning the affection. It is that sort of love that applies specifically to babies, young children and some disabled people; although we all need a bit of it from time to time! Reiki *is* Motherly Love, and its role here is to help us understand the true needs of those we care for, to channel the love to them when necessary, and to help us know when we have to let go.

Brotherly Love

The love of equals. Brothers and Sisters in the widest sense. It would include the love not just between siblings but between members of a group, work force, sports team, etc. True brotherly love has no limitations, but all too often brotherly love is restricted to that aspect of life that the brothers (team, etc) have in common: For example if a team mate finds that another member of his squad is having an affair with his partner, which love 'wins'? Having said that, having parents, a hobby or a cause in common can really bring two or more people together. That common interest becomes a resonance, a genuine bond of love.

Reiki itself can be the bond between 'brothers'. We are, after all, following in the footsteps of monastic brothers. Being able to give our 'brother' a Reiki treatment gives us a valuable additional way to demonstrate our love for someone.

Community Spirit

Extend the concept of Brotherly Love to a larger group and we have Community Spirit. Here the common interest might be something much broader than a particular hobby. 'Community' is typically a village or a neighbourhood, but could be a group of individuals or families that:

* Share the same nationality, culture or religious background (e.g. Ex-pats in Hong Kong or Chinatown in a Western city)

* Have a common aim or purpose (e.g. spiritual quest)

As with each aspect of human love, there are limitations. All too often the common interest that leads to the establishment of a community can isolate that group from other aspects of humanity: a Jewish quarter (for example) can become a ghetto, a religious community can become a fanatical cult. Within any true community however is a spirit that binds them together, which supports the members through all manner of hardships. Love. Within bounds maybe, but a powerful force that helps many of us feel we belong - a fairly fundamental need of us all!

The 'Reiki Community' is growing rapidly - at all levels. From local sharing groups to the International Community that embraces *all* practitioners of Reiki. Some like to 'ring-fence' their part of this wider Reiki Community, restricting it to students of a given Master or 'type' of Reiki. This is their choice. To me however, if we practice Reiki or some other healing art then we *are* brothers and belong to a single community, almost by definition. This is certainly how many saw it in the English county of Northamptonshire, where I used to live: I helped to create 'The Rose Community' which embraced all those living and/or working holistically. From Organic Food Co-operative to Spiritual or Reiki Healer, from Palmist to Yoga Teacher, from Arts & Leisure officer to Meditation group. *All* part of the spiritual community. How can it, in truth, be any different?

Love of Nature

As a country lad, brought up helping my dad in a large garden, the world of plants, trees and flowers has always been a fascination to me and for me. I've often thought that the future of our society lies in villages and rural settlements that understand the natural world. Reiki has further heightened my appreciation of all things natural. The magic of seeds sprouting in spring, the ebb and flow of waves on a beach, the wonder of a sunset and beauty of a butterfly. Yes, this awe of the natural world is another form of love. In our environment we see the power and mystical side of life. The more the natural world is explored, the more amazing it becomes. We love nature by allowing it to embrace us in all its glory. We love nature by praising its abundance and magnificence.

There is no separation between Reiki and nature. Both ARE the Universal life on which we depend. I was lucky (!) enough to do my Reiki II and Masters on the edge of the English Peak District. With the hills and dales as a backdrop, and the winds to share our learning space, the true nature of Reiki was very much in evidence. Whenever possible I include a walk along canal, river or forest within all my Reiki classes. After the experience of an attunement, there's little to match a country walk to help us feel connected to life itself.

Making Friends with the Wind

Suppose we're on a walk and wind is blowing strongly in our face. Instead of thinking 'the wind's against us' we welcome the freshness of the breeze, we feel the tingling of our skin. Let it blow away any thoughts that disturb your peace. Feel your mind cleared by the wind, all the dead-wood blown away, leaving you feeling at peace AND enlivened.

Perhaps it seems hard going walking into the wind, so let the wind help you! Lean into the wind with head and shoulders and allow it to pick you up - like a kite. You now only need effort to move forward, the wind is carrying your weight for you. Watch the birds circling around and, like them, fly.

Listen to the whooshing of the wind in your ears. What's it saying? Is there a message for you? Or is it a soothing sound, easing your mind into the natural environment around you. Listen. Make friends with the wind and it will support you. BE with the energy of life.

Self Love

Give yourself a hug. Yes, now! Don't you deserve it? Of course you do! When first facing up to the fact that my romantic failures were of my own making, I had a thought: *If there's nobody here to love me, and there's nobody for me to love - why don't I love myself?* Logical isn't it. I also realised that if I didn't enjoy my own company, why should anybody else enjoy it? From those thoughts in my late 20's I gradually stopped clinging to unrealistic romances. Reiki gave me a wonderful tool with which to practice the self love I was obviously in need of. We cannot always rely on some other person being around to give us their love. The ability to love ourselves takes much pressure off our partners, it frees us all up to BE our true self. It is a vital part of taking responsibility for our own lives and our own feelings. Our true self that is, our inner self. Self love is about connecting to our soul and making *it* feel wanted. Doing that allows love to flow within and around us - far from being a selfish act, it is one that frees us to truly love life. As Reiki becomes part of our day to day life, so we are always loving ourselves. In doing so we are enabled to love others more too.

Romantic/Erotic Love

One of the best descriptions of *true* romantic love I've come across is in the book 'The Shared Heart' by Barry & Joyce Vissell. Here, for the first time I came across the notion that our special relationships with one another are also our relationship with God. If divine love is becoming One with the divine, then true romantic love is when two people become one - in mind, body and soul. Erotic love is the merging not just of two bodies, but the intimate joining of two minds and two souls inter-twining. The height of passion *is* divine. Being truly in love romantically is often the first, perhaps the only taste, of divine love that many people experience. The bliss of love-making, the ecstasy of union *is* the ultimate love - when we surrender to each other and loose ourselves in something bigger than any of us . . . Universal Love.

Relationships are a path to our reunion with God, and Reiki helps tremendously in understanding and accepting our partner emotionally and mentally. Physically it brings us together. Spiritually it enables us to connect at a far deeper level. Relationships and romantic love are part of the spiritual journey for most of us. The Universe does, after all, provide for *all* our needs!

2 - The System of Healing

To me, Reiki just *IS* . . . and the aim of this book is to help others see and experience this broad perspective. However, Reiki has acquired various labels. In this chapter, some of these are put into perspective. Then we'll explore the heart of Reiki - don't worry, I'll keep this bit about labels as brief as possible!

Reiki Healing, as opposed to 'Reiki the Energy' should perhaps be more correctly called 'The Usui System' or 'The Usui System of Natural Healing' after its founder (at least in modern times) Mikau Usui. Quite what constitutes Reiki Healing, or even The Usui System is subject to considerable debate. Is it what Usui himself taught? Maybe, but what *is* that? Or it is the wide range of different healing practices *based* on Usui's teachings and using Reiki Energy? An increasing number of Reiki teachers are rising above the definition debate and just getting on with what Reiki is to them.

In this book I tend to use the term Reiki to mean the energy (in the broadest sense). I'll use the term 'Reiki Healing' to mean any healing practice which owes its origins to Usui's work. When I use just the term 'Healing' I mean not just Reiki Healing, but any form of natural healing that does not depend upon manipulations, medicine (natural or otherwise) or tools. In most circumstances there is little, if any, difference between the different forms of healing. There is, after all, only one Universal Energy and it is this that all forms of healing access. What differs is the type of training, if any, that the practitioners have undergone.

I Remember!

We talk of teaching and learning Reiki (or Reiki Healing), as if it's another school subject like Geography or French. It's not really like that. Reiki isn't a set of facts and figures to be remembered. Learning Reiki is more like learning to walk or swim. Yes, we have to put the effort into practice, and it can help to have someone show us how, but it's more about *allowing* our body to *just DO it!*

Think about the subjects we learn at school, some we take to, some we don't. In a few we're a *natural*, others we just can't get into at all. OK, sometimes this is a function of the teacher, but more likely it's just that subject doesn't resonate with our way of thinking and being. I took readily to maths and the science subjects but couldn't get into languages at all at secondary school. Why was this? Probably because they 'weren't me'.

I *did* take to Reiki - obviously, or I wouldn't be writing this! Why? Because it seems so natural. It's not as if I'm learning something new, more that I'm *remembering* what I've always known.

Universal truths *are* within us. The realities of life are part of our inherent make up - it is from them that we are made, after all. Thus, when we're told them, they *should* seem right and natural.

Contrast this with our struggle to comprehend other subjects. Conventional learning can be *such* hard work . . . but only if we're trying to force something into our mind which doesn't belong there! If you're finding this is true of Reiki, if what you're being taught doesn't ring true, then question your Master. If they can't reassure you, change your Master.

In any subject, a sure sign of a job well done by a teacher is a class of faces that, from time to time, light up. A smile that says "Ah! I remember". In Reiki and other such subjects, this is doubly so. Reiki is about connecting us to our innate wisdom, it is about helping us to remember all the wonderful things about life that we *do* already know.

Yes, at times the conscious mind could well rebel against the unconventional ideas that come with the enlightenment process. But the inner self *knows* that the truth will out eventually. Learning Reiki Healing, when taught in the spirit of Reiki, assists this process. It is a re-awakening. A remembering. No more, no less.

Reiki - Without Rules

Levels of Reiki

Different branches of Reiki divide up the teaching of The Usui System in different ways. Although recent research has identified a written Manual used by Usui, there is no single agreed 'System'. There is however some agreement on the following levels of basic Reiki training:

* First Degree - Focusing on 'hands-on' healing.

* Second Degree - When Reiki Symbols are first taught, and their use for absent healing.

* Masters (or Third Degree) - Covering an additional symbol (or symbols), and how to 'pass on' Reiki through attunements.

Sometimes a level '3A' is offered meaning 'Masters - but not for teaching'. Other branches of Reiki also offer additional levels of training, some based on particular Buddhist schools of training. Don't be put off by this. After all, since when did all English teachers teach the same system in the same way? There is great variety in Reiki teaching and this is perhaps one of its strengths. For, with so many different 'Systems' of Reiki, there's far more likely to be one that's right for each of us.

In this book, I use the 'Three Degree' System given above, simply because that's how I teach it, and that's what works for me. But there are no rules. I see Reiki training in the Usui System as a means to helping students access the Reiki energy within themselves. If there is a distinction between the different levels of training, it is this: First Degree (Reiki I) is about healing at the physical level, Second Degree (Reiki II) is about healing at the emotional and mental level and Masters (Reiki III) is about healing at the spiritual level. At each level we explore the energy of Reiki within a different level of ourselves - body, then mind, then soul. But, as someone is bound to point out, these three are inseparable - so please don't get attached to these distinctions!

Learning the System

If learning Reiki is about exploring Reiki, the energy, where then does the 'system of healing' fit in? There is much debate on this question! Some Reiki Masters insist that 'The System' is sacrosanct and that sticking to defined details of the physical practice and transmission of Reiki are vital. Vital to what, I wonder. One difficulty with this approach, as we shall see when we look into the history of Reiki (Chapter 4), is that there is no global agreement on which definition of the Usui System is the right one.

Does it really matter which version of Reiki, which set of 'rules' we follow? This is a question you will need to answer for yourself. My experience is that it doesn't matter. Given that the aim is to experience the energy of Reiki healing, then any system, technique or method that facilitates the flow of energy is valid. Reiki seems to flow whichever definition you use. Reiki healing occurs whichever school of Reiki we might align ourselves to.

This may not help those seeking a Reiki teacher! Choosing a Reiki Master is discussed in more detail in Chapter 30 - after we've explored what being a Master is all about. For now, however, a few tips on choosing a Master for First (or Second) Degree:

* Decide what it is you're hoping to get from learning Reiki. Why are you doing it? Don't worry if you've no clear rational answer to this question. "Because I *have* to" is probably the best reason possible.

* Be aware of the work you may have already done on your path. What else have you done by way of self development, therapies, philosophical research, etc.

* Identify what you feel you're able to give to your Reiki training, in terms of time, money and other commitments.

i.e. before choosing your Master have a sense of where Reiki might fit into your life. Then read the leaflets of a number of teachers, talk to them and their students. Get a feel for how they see Reiki Healing. Are they likely to be able to relate to your background and your needs? Are they going to be around to support you after the course? Do you feel comfortable with them and drawn to them? If you are, then their system of Reiki is likely to be in tune with your needs. Basically, allow your intuition to guide you.

* Talk to prospective teachers (on the phone or in person) and ask them each '20 questions' - to reflect your concerns and needs.

* Just Do It . . . and let 'fate' decide.

3 - A Way of Life

By now it will be clear to many of you that to categorise Reiki as a system of healing or as a therapy is to miss the point about Reiki Healing. Those of us who have lived with Reiki, or rather lived *in* Reiki - and let Reiki live in us, *know* that it is beyond any such categorisation. Yes, Reiki *is* a healing therapy, but the formal system of healing is but a first step on a much broader healing path. When we allow Reiki to become part of us, it does so with no restrictions. I'd like now to give some example of what Reiki is as a way of life - the energy of life in action in our normal activities in a human society:

* Community Spirit. That buzz when a group of individuals get together for a shared activity. Whether it's a community fete, a sporting event or a group of friends at a barbeque. When there *is* a common purpose, when the event takes on an energy of its own, then all participating have allowed Community Spirit to live in and through them. This is Reiki in action. Sometimes consciously - as some individuals make a conscious effort to support their friends and neighbours, often unconsciously . . . as we all just 'go with the flow' and allow the whole to be greater than the sum of the parts.

* A zest for life. How is it that some people nearly always have a natural smile on their face and are genuinely willing and able to share their time and efforts with those in need? Such individuals just seem able to enjoy themselves, they sail through life. This is going with the flow and is possible for anybody . . . once they are in tune with their inner self. This is the Reiki way of Life. Reiki *is* enthusiasm, a joy of life and living. The more willing and able we are to live this way, the easier it comes. Yes, it probably is about having a positive attitude and often this needs to be learnt, but those with a zest for life live it lightly - like angels . . they don't take themselves, or anything else, too seriously.

* The Lord of The Dance. Any free and natural expression of life.

Reiki - Without Rules

Singing, dancing, playing musical instruments are all ways of allowing the energy of life to live in and through us. When we become immersed in our favourite concerto, or join in with our favourite songs we connect with the energy of the music, of the performer and of the mood of the piece.

* Our Inner Child. Picture the wonder of a child when he sees a waterfall or a bird for the first time. See the bright, lively, nature of a child at play: exploring, creating, allowing his sense of fun to guide him as he learns to live. Why should this ever die? It doesn't have to! The Inner Child, or Playful Spirit, is one aspect of our Inner Self . . . allow them to play and they'll brighten up your days no end!

* Arts & Crafts. The creating of anything, be it to use or look at, is a special activity. The closer we become involved with the materials involved, the more we allow our intuitive side expression, the more we sense an inner guidance to our work. Many famous artists and crafts folks are often described as being channels for Gods work, but this is something we can all do.

All of these are examples of 'being', of living to love and loving to live. Reiki Healing allows the Reiki Energy to live in us. By committing to this process as a way of life, we become true to ourselves. Through this book and through learning and practising Reiki, I hope to enable you too to find fulfilment in your life. Certainly many of my students report having taken great steps in this direction.

Evolution

Reiki helps us to become aware of how we react to life. As we do so, we can see that we're in a process of change - from being basically animals in behaviour to being whole spiritual beings. Our way of life reflects this. The above enlightened ways of living contrast, often markedly, with typical behaviour in society. For example:

In many of our actions we still react instinctively - we let our animal natures determine our actions. Such reactions may be part of our ancestry but, as we progress towards spirituality, they have little place. Part of our re-alignment is the reprogramming of our base response mechanisms: replacing our 'selfish gene' approach to life with a 'soul purpose' one. Letting our inner self decide what we should do in a given circumstance, for the greater good . . . rather than what's necessary for the survival of our species.

One such animal instinct is to 'fight or flight' when faced with a dangerous situation. As animals under threat our ancient mind either fights the perceived danger . . . or runs away from it. This nature is still predominant in our behaviour today - when we see something we don't like the look of we'll either lash out at it or turn away from it. Often, without realising it, we 'fight or flight' when put in a situation that makes us uncomfortable.

But there is a third option: to *face* the situation. The old 'fight or flight' is governed by fear. Now we are learning that there is nothing to fear except fear itself (e.g. Susan Jeffers 'Feel the Fear and Do It Anyway'). OK, *sometimes* it's prudent to stand our ground and fight our corner . . . or to run for cover . . . but often not. As we learn to live in Reiki, so we're able to face the skeletons in our cupboards. By tuning into our higher selves we can raise ourselves above our animal natures - we no longer need to fight for our 'territory', for we now know that 'possession' and 'ownership' are human concepts with little meaning. When we give love to a situation then the sense of sharing takes over. Instead of 'tribal warfare' we now seek a community of consensus . . . living in harmony with ourselves as diverse individuals.

The sexual urge is another area which we begin to see differently. As we become more aware, so we recognise the difference between animal lust (the selfish gene wanting to procreate) and a genuine spiritual connection. As we outgrow the former, so we learn to see beneath the physical attraction to our 'soul mate'. We see how we are brought together not so much to propagate the human genes but to assist each other on our spiritual journeys.

Throughout this book we explore what Reiki is within a wide range of aspects of human life. As a system of healing it is a powerful tool.

Reiki - Without Rules

As an energy it is within and around everything we see, touch and otherwise sense. With practice it can become a way of life.

THE HISTORY OF REIKI

4 - Can any history be true?

History, by definition, is concerned with the past, things that have already happened. How we perceive those past people and events depends largely on our intent in studying the past. Do we need to know the history of Reiki in order to feel the benefits of it? Probably not! However, we are talking of an holistic approach to life, of wholeness. Thus, the next few, short, chapters are included for the sake of completeness . . . and to help our understanding of how Reiki came to be with us in the way it is.

A wide range of stories are told about Reiki and its origins. So much so that we have to wonder what the truth is. But is it realistic to expect a single history, agreed by all, to be found and presented? Given human nature, such a coming together of the different schools of Reiki is unlikely. Facts will always be distorted by beliefs. Opinions will always be introduced when interpreting information from another time.

History is merely our human minds' attempt to describe things that have happened in a way that explains how we see things now and how we'd like to see them develop. As anybody who has truly experienced Reiki will tell you, Reiki transcends time. The history of Reiki is inextricably tied up with Reiki present and Reiki in the future. Anybody who tries to tell you otherwise, who insists on certain facts about Reiki, has missed the point. History is a human invention. It is unreal. It doesn't *really* matter.

History, like any other written or screened presentation, has an author. Whilst it may well be *based* on what actually happened, an historical account probably tells us more about that author than about the event being described. When reviewing the various, often conflicting, histories of Reiki that are now available, we may be tempted to ask which is fact and which fiction?

Fact or Fiction

It is often said that truth is stranger than fiction. Looking at the recent film offerings and TV schedules would seem to confirm this. 'Real life' dramas set in fire-stations, 'Great Escapes' from horrific accidents, "Titanic", etc. Here are real examples of individual humans facing their fears, finding that inner strength. Through life we learn and grow.

So what role fiction? If it helps us to relate to reality, does it matter whether we call in fact or fiction? Besides, the distinction is often lost. Much drama is 'based' on fact. Much fact is dramatised. Where do you draw the line? *Why* draw a line? So long as it helps us to see something anew, to broaden our mind and grow. What is perhaps more important is the degree of truth in the book, programme, film, etc. It's the ability to connect us into *our* inner truth that makes a bit of writing or screen presentation 'good' or otherwise. i.e. it needs to be *inspired.* True genius expresses itself through the arts *and* through science - Einstein and Tolkien for example. Inspired fiction has as much truth in it as factual works. On our path to enlightenment we can find much to draw us onwards and upwards in novels - of all categories. I write this having just read Clive Barker's "Imajica". A truly inspired work of art, bringing out so many truths of life - the role of the Goddess, the circle of magic . . . and how they affect our relationships.

Again, many are going to ask "What has this got to do with Reiki?" Again I answer "Much"! Just as Reiki, the Universal Life-force Energy has many other names from different religious, philosophical and mystical traditions, so too does it have fictional counterparts. Reiki, besides being Prana and Chi, is also Imajica and 'The Force' of Star Wars. Throughout literature we have the concept of an all prevailing power, and energy that will always bring *its* order to bear. Whatever genre of book, whatever period of fictional work, this deeper truth can be found. Why? *Because it IS within and around all of us* . . . and a good author is inspired by it . . . even in a 'history' book!

The conclusion? *Avoid the temptation to label any given account of Reiki's history as 'fact' or 'fiction'.* Each version is, or at least was, true to the writer when they wrote it. Each provides us with some pointer as to what various researchers felt was important about Usui and Reiki. Some stories will ring more true with us than others. That's the nature of any history. It's not worth losing any sleep over.

The Usui Story

Up until the mid 1990's the story usually told of Reiki's beginning was that Usui taught at a Christian seminary in Japan. When asked about healing he embarked on a world tour to seek out the truth about healing. During that search he found some ancient Sanskrit texts which he couldn't interpret but which he knew were important. He meditated on these during a fast and retreat up a sacred mountain once back in Japan. It was during this time that he 'received' wisdom and suddenly understood the ancient writings . . . from which the Reiki symbols came. It was from this experience that Usui developed his system of healing known as Reiki.

During the 90's this story was researched by a number of Reiki Masters and found to contain many inaccuracies. There is, for example, no evidence that Usui taught at a Christian school or that he travelled to the West. It is, however, likely that he did start practising and teaching Reiki after a retreat on a Japanese sacred mountain. We're also fairly sure that Usui was well versed in Buddhism and it's likely that the ancient text he had revealed to him were of Buddhist origins. Whilst this probably doesn't matter too much, this background does give us some insight into Usui and thus to the origins of Reiki Healing . . . and its true nature.

So, why say that Usui was a Christian when he probably wasn't? Why the untruths? Maybe there were misunderstandings. Maybe embellishments at the time Reiki came to the West. Almost certainly they were not propagated with any intent to deceive. On the contrary. It seems reasonable that the stories of Usui links to Christianity and to The West were told to make it easier for Westerners to accept Reiki. It is likely that few, if any, of those propagating the original Western version of the story were aware of their inaccuracy. Whatever. It is all now history. The important thing is that Reiki came to West . . . and thank God it did!

5 - The changing face of Reiki

Having said that history doesn't matter, in attempting to help people understand and appreciate Reiki, it is useful to review the roots of Reiki . . . at least in general terms. In this book few details are given. Specific facts and figures apply only at the time and in the place that you hear or see them, and even then they often need to be questioned. For those interested in dates and 'facts', 'Reiki Fire' by Frank Petter provides some research results.

Some 'facts' about Reiki and its history are generally agreed:

* Usui 'found' it in the late 1800's. We now know that he was well versed in Buddhism. It is likely that he 'rediscovered' some ancient wisdom rather than found or invented anything new.

* Usui passed his teachings on to Hayashi (amongst others) and Hayashi passed it on to Takata, amongst others. Quite what we mean by 'it' or 'his teachings' is open to debate.

* It was Takata who brought Reiki to the West.

More than that is difficult to say with any certainty.

We know that Hayashi used Reiki in clinical circumstances, so it is likely that he adapted what he was taught to allow for such an environment.

We know that the worlds of Usui (Japan in the 1890's and early 1900's) and Takata (Hawaii in the 1930's & 'the West' up to 1980) were very different in character and attitudes. It is quite likely that Takata made changes to what she was taught in order to have Reiki accepted in the USA. And why not? Reiki is a living tradition, it is adaptable to suit the time and place that it is brought into practice.

We know that Takata taught 21 (some say 22) students to Masters level (between 1970 and her death in 1980) and that it is from these teachers that most (but not all) Western Reiki teachers can trace their lineage. But these students were taught over a period of 10 years and some 30 - 40 years after Takata had become a Reiki Master. During this time Takata herself would have been growing in her understanding of Reiki. Any teaching Reiki Master will tell you that through each attunement they give, they grow. Add to that the fact that each student of Reiki will read into it their own interpretations and relate it to their own background and experiences. We can see how a diverse range of ideas on what Reiki is and how it should be taught has come about.

Usui's path

Research into Usui during the 1990's suggests that his retreat up Mount Kurama came at the time of considerable personal problems. He was confused, he was in need of divine guidance. It was this that enabled him to hear his inner guidance and to reflect with a great openness on the ancient, sacred, texts. His genuine desire to find truth was rewarded with a truly enlightening experience . . . from which the world of Reiki Healing has developed. It is to this beginning that we need to look, to appreciate what Reiki is. Usui himself 'found' the hidden wisdom when he needed it most. Reiki resulted from a personal growth experience. Rediscovering the healing secrets of the universal energy of life was a major step on Usui's own spiritual journey. His commitment to the journey brought about a healing system that is helping to heal millions around the world . . . and thus the world itself. Our commitment to Our spiritual journey will likewise heal our lives . . . and continue the human awakening process that Usui started.

After saying that, it hardly seems to matter which lineage any of us are on . . . nor make any difference precisely how we teach or practice Reiki. If we are to follow in Usui's footsteps with his system, we should surely do so with his spirit . . . a determination to find peace and fulfilment in our own lives . . . by seeking out truth and doing whatever we *know* we have to.

Reiki - Without Rules

If that still isn't enough to raise Reiki from the list of 'alternative therapies', perhaps this question might: Did Usui use a massage couch? In the midst of the earthquake hit towns that we're told he worked in? . It seems unlikely! One thing is clear: since Usui's first Reiki healing, Reiki has been used in many, many, different ways. It is an ever changing practice . . . like life itself really.

6 - Here and now

So, as we move further into the new millennium, where is Reiki now? A good question! Judging by its increasing appearance in journals and on TV and radio it is one of the most rapidly growing therapies of the time . . . and that amidst a huge increase in people who use Complementary Therapy (of all sorts) as well as, and increasingly instead of, conventional medicine. There is little doubt that Reiki Healing has grabbed the public imagination.

But is it a fad, a passing phase, born of hype and marketing pressure? Unlikely, since despite the efforts of a few, the interest in Reiki has spread largely by word of mouth. Its popularity increases because it *does* make a difference.

Increasingly Reiki is being shown to be effective in tacking a wide range of conditions. Increasingly those in conventional medical professions are recognising its value and accepting its use. True, there are still many who insist on proof through clinical trial and who demand to know *how* it works. But those who have experienced the benefits don't really care about all this. Besides, the news from 'New Science' is that typical Reiki effects are by no means inconsistent with sub-atomic physics and the latest theories of morphogenetic resonance and the like.

I find it interesting that the Buddhist background to Reiki has come to light at just the time that such philosophies have become accepted to many in the West. As we search for meaning in our lives, so concepts such as 'spirituality', 'awareness' and 'enlightenment' become attractive and we are willing and able to face the challenges of living in tune with the principles of Buddha . . . or our own chosen ascended Master.

A sense of injustice

Many honest, caring, people in the world today are fighting (in some way, often peacefully) for a cause they hold dear to them. Their role in life *is* to run charities for the homeless, raise funds to research into cancer - or some lesser known disease, or campaign for those living under repressive regimes. Most do so out of an inner sense of injustice, of *knowing* that the current status quo is not truthful. Their path, their lesson, is to explore this situation, to learn what it is like to suffer, to experience the frustration of being a minority, or being un-heard, un-cared for.

What has this got to do with Reiki? Everything! All paths are paths on our spiritual journey. Whatever we end up doing in and with our lives we do so to satisfy our soul - our inner self. i.e., and some won't thank me for saying this, what we do, we do for ourselves - not for the victims our cause supports. They merely reflect our inner needs. This is not to say that campaigners are behaving selfishly. Not at all. They (we!) do what we *have* to do. For the greater good. By playing our part in the cosmic and global game of life, so we learn our lesson and we help other healing processes to occur.

Take one campaign that can claim a relevance to Reiki. The plight of Tibet. The people of Tibet, home of much Buddhist wisdom, are under the rule of the Chinese. Despite being against UN resolutions, the Chinese continue to severely restrict traditional Tibetan cultural and religious activity. The teachings that we in Reiki circles see as so important are denied to the descendants of those who first taught them.

The Dalai Lama continues his work in exile. In India, Tibetans continue to teach and learn their culture, their inheritance. Why can they not do so in their own country? What can *we* do about it?

What I'm doing is to raise awareness of the situation. To bring the matter into public consciousness. With Reiki we can add our prayers to those of the Tibetans.

I make no judgement in this matter. We are all learning the lessons we have to learn - the campaigners, the Chinese and the Tibetans themselves. The way forward is to rise above an emotional reaction to the situation. To be open and honest in raising awareness of the facts . . . and encouraging those who are able to make a difference to do so without fear. In the UK, for example, a postcard campaign encouraged PM Tony Blair to raise the Tibetan issue on a visit to China. It was not done in the glare of publicity (that was probably not appropriate), but steps are now being taken. The path to truth is often a long and lonely one. Next time you feel that times are hard, that life is not fair, spare a thought for the Tibetans (and other refugees) who do not even have their home land to feel despair in. I don't mean feel sorry for them (pity serves little purpose) I mean tune into the essence of the Tibetan culture, feel the resonance between their Buddhist practices and ours, *be* with our common lineage. How deep is *your* love?

Try this visualisation/meditation:

Look closely at 'Our Spiritual Lineage' (below) and include yourself on the diagram - under Reiki and/or under your own religious branch. Imagine too that under the Tibetan Buddhist arm are the Dalai Lama and Tibetan Buddhists - some following their practice in exile, others in secret (and with risk) in their homeland. Picture them in your mind. Monks without a monastery. Individuals seeking truth. See the connection between us, our common bond in the teachings of Buddha. The teachings of truth. The path. Our path. All of us, wherever we fit on the Spiritual Lineage. Allow the connections to be made, stronger, deeper as the higher truth beneath all religion is felt in our hearts and souls. We are One. As our spirits connect so we know that we are not alone, neither in this world nor in others beyond human comprehension. Let you mind rest on an image of a Master you feel important to you. Perhaps it's Buddha or Jesus, Sai Baba or Sogyal Rinpoche, Mother Meera or Isis. Through that image allow yourself to connect to the innate wisdom and beauty that IS a true Master. They are One, We are all One.

Although the plight of Tibet and its people and the increasing use of Reiki (and other holistic therapies), would seem disconnected, both reflect the here and now. They are both examples of the realities that we as humans live with. It is in this context that we learn, practise and teach Reiki. For, unless it can help us *in* this world, what's the point of it?

Our Spiritual Lineage

Very much simplified!

With apologies to followers of spiritual/religious leaders
not mentioned below

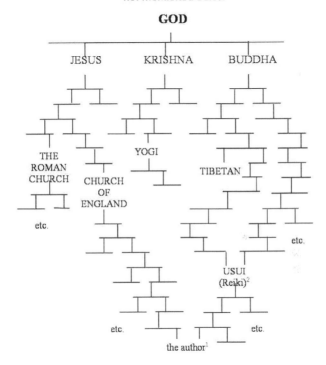

Most of us are influenced by many different sources of spiritual wisdom

1. The author was brought up and confirmed into the Church of England
2. Recent research suggests that Usui (and thus Reiki) was influenced by a number of different branches of Buddhism.

Getting back to our roots

Reiki - Without Rules

7 - The future

So where is this trend taking us? Are we all going to become Buddhists? Not very likely! For as Reiki lives within us, we rise above the need for religions or predetermined rules by which to live. As we connect to our inner/higher selves, we live beyond beliefs. We become free of the 'shoulds' and 'oughts' of our conditioning and allow the love, the light, to live in us and through us. We automatically do what we have to do, for our own good and for the greater good. As more and more people reach this stage of personal growth, so society flows more naturally. As we learn to make no distinction between ourselves, other people and life itself, so we find all our needs are satisfied and our lives become more joyous, more fulfilling.

OK, this could take some decades or maybe centuries, but this is the trend visible to all with eyes open enough to see it . . . or maybe that's just another belief. It doesn't matter! Once we have allowed Reiki, or some other path or tool, to reconnect our mind/body with our soul, then we will not need beliefs or theories. We'll just get on and enjoy life!

Like writing history, any attempt to predict the future is risky. But at least by doing what we know we have to do now, we'll be doing our bit to bring about the future that we need!

Many are drawn to Reiki by a vision of a 'heaven on earth'. We are shown how life *could* be and that vision gives us the courage and determination to change our lives in order to bring about that vision. But it's a vision that cannot be described in detail, or predicted. For then it becomes a product of the human conscious mind, a plan, an attempt to control. As soon as we do that, we've lost the vision.

Our Future

Perhaps the only thing about our future we can say with any

certainty, is that *our* lives in the future is up to us. If there's one thing Reiki teaches us it's that our personal life, and how we view it, is our responsibility and nobody else's. Thus, the best way to ensure a future that is happy and fulfilling is to *be* happy now. Reiki helps us in that process. It will help us sort our dreams from reality and *know* which opportunities are worth taking. Focusing our love in the moment creates the futures we need.

REIKI HEALING

- THE BASICS

8 - What do you Need to know?

In terms of facts and set procedures you need very little, if any, to practice Reiki successfully. There are No Rules. Reiki is not only the Universal Energy but the Ultimate Wisdom. The Reiki knows best what needs to happen. All we have to do, is to let it!

Sometimes its not as easy as that. To 'just let it happen' often means letting go of many preconceived ideas and conditioned ways of thinking and behaving. Thus, to be most successful with Reiki requires an open mind and a willingness to surrender to it. The more we fight it the more we'll suffer. Much of this book is aimed at helping our conscious mind to accept what's happening and to surrender gracefully to the power and wisdom of the Universe . . . to the will of God.

If that idea grates with you it could mean many things. Perhaps you just like to be in control? Is that really healthy and best for you? As we learn to work with Reiki and to trust in its power, so we learn that, unlike any*body* or any*thing,* Reiki *does* have our interest at heart. Reiki knows what we *need.* This may not be what we *want,* but eventually we find that life does flow far more naturally the more we listen to our inner/higher voice . . . and let the Reiki work within us.

Knowing, in Reiki terms, is thus not about an intellectual understanding but about an inner knowing. The more we use Reiki the more our confidence in that inner sense grows. Gradually we learn to listen to the inner voice instead of our nagging intellectual mind. The change-over process can take many years . . . our patience is often tried in the process! There are many old notions and emotional attachments to let go of

Argggh!

There are times when this process of letting go gets a bit much. There could well be times when we feel like death warmed up, when none of our visualisations or bits of relaxing music work. There are times when we feel that it's just not fair! We may *know* that all this hard work is for the best, that we *will* feel much better once we have let go of whatever it is our old self clings to. For that's all(!) such times are - a reluctance to let go of our old ways of living and thinking. But that doesn't make such times any easier to cope with. When we feel feverish and achy, when we've a tickly cough, can't sleep, can't eat and our mind is in a state unlike anything we've ever experienced before, then we do wonder what the hell we've got ourselves into. If this is how you feel as you read this, Bless You! . . . it's how I feel as I write this chapter, so I *do* know how you feel!

So when we just want to curl up and do nothing, but even that leaves us restless, what can we do? We need to know some simples methods to help us relax and release whatever is holding us back . . . to complement the flow of Reiki. The following are suitable for beginners to Reiki and to 'experts' alike:

1. Write! Which is what I'm doing now. Get your thoughts and feelings out. It will do *something* to ease the tension. Or draw - even if it's only a scribble.

2. Curl up - with your favourite cuddly toy, pet . . . or lover if you have one. If not, love yourself. You *are* going through major changes, so need to focus energy on yourself.

Reiki - Without Rules

3. Get some fresh air - even if only standing at an (open) back door watching the birds, insects, plants and clouds. It reminds us that nature doesn't think about things - it reminds us that life just IS.

4. Get some exercise - walk, dance, yoga - whatever has some attraction to you. 20 minutes with mind focused on this activity will again detach our worries and doubts . . . and get the energy flowing around our body to release the toxins.

Maybe we're tried all of these and still feel frustrated and fed up. Umm. Let the Universe guide you - maybe you're led to watch TV and your favourite film *does* hold your attention and give you some positive ideas. Or maybe you know that you really do need help and a name comes to mind . . . someone who will at least know how you're feeling and help you to feel not alone.

If possible, just surrender to it and let the Universe do what it can to help you - during the second full day of my crisis, I had three unexpected callers and a lovely positive E-Mail! If we *are* helpless and *need* help, the Universe *will* provide. This experience was just before Christmas, so the idea of a helpless babe was certainly around and one I could relate to. The third caller was selling Prize Draw tickets for local Cancer & Cerebral Palsy groups - a clear reminder that many are worse of than I. My 'rough patch' lasted only a few days, for many the sense of helplessness lasts months or many years. Those living though war or famine have to cope with on-going and very real challenges. Perspective is a valuable tool in helping us see that things could be much, much, worse - or at least that we're not alone in our experience.

When in pain, try this:

Choose a piece of music that seems to fit your mood. Sit or lie comfortably and listen to the sounds, allow your mind to follow its rhythm and tone. Notice any particular ache or pain in your body and place your hands there . . . wherever - eyes, stomach, knees, etc. As you hands gently press the place, allow your attention to focus on that part of you. Feel the heat (or tingle, or cold or whatever) begin to spread . . . and express how it feels. If it's an intense pain, then grimace, shout out "Ouch", scream if that helps to release the pain. Hold that place until the pain has gone or subsided. Repeat on any other ache or pain, allowing any suppressed anger or fear to come out in tears or sighs. It's better out than in! Release and find relief. Use the music. With slow passages feel a calmness flow through you, let it ease away your troubles. With more energetic music, feel the healing energy rushing through you, flushing out any blocks in your system. The flow of the music, the flow of the healing energy of Reiki are one, cleansing your system, leaving you feeling refreshed, freer.

[Note: this exercise, like most, can be attempted by anybody, but those with Reiki experience (or similar) are likely to find them easier and more profound. If you practise Reiki, then do a self treatment to get into the exercise. If you're practising Second Degree, use the symbols over you and/or the subject of the exercise]

We are all Healers

It is true that we, humans beings at the turn of the millennium, are still intellectual beings. Often we *do* need theories and models of healing, of the world, before our conscious minds can accept. That's OK. So long as we're aware that models are just that. Constructs of the human mind aimed at helping those same minds to understand the world around us. Eventually, as we tune into the true beauty and wonder of the world, we become content to experience the world as it is. As Reiki helps us to free our mind of all its conditioning, so we naturally 'go with the flow'. Then, we don't need to understand! All we need to know (which we do, deep down) is that we *are* all healers!

First Degree Reiki courses aim to help us accept this. The remainder of this section of the book covers the topics which I usually include in Reiki I training. Some focus on enabling first-hand experience of Reiki energy, some at putting Reiki Healing into a broader perspective . . . and some, aim to placate our questioning mind!

9 - An inherent ability: channelling

We are all healers. We all have some inherent ability to heal ourselves and others. We must have, otherwise we'd never get better from sores, cuts, coughs and colds.

Think too of how we put our head in our hands when we have a headache, hold our stomach when our guts are churning and rub better our children's grazes. In each case we are focusing our attention on the bit that hurts and thus encouraging the healing process at that point.

It's useful to compare our healing ability with say our athletic ability. We can all run and jump to some extent, but few have the natural ability of the Olympic medallists Daley Thompson or Linford Christie. Thus only a few individuals are able to heal others instinctively. Most of us need to be coached, need to have our abilities enhanced through appropriate exercises - this is what happens in Reiki classes. First Degree Reiki brings out our natural healing ability. It helps us to recognise and have confidence in our own ability to heal. After that, the more we practice, the more we allow the healing energy to flow, the more that ability will grow.

The 'giving' of a Reiki 'treatment' is often described as a 'channelling' of the Universal Energy. It is, but not in the sense of a *physical* channel. A Reiki healer does not channel energy from 'out there' *into* the person 'receiving' the treatment. Reiki, being Universal, is already everywhere. It doesn't need to 'come' and 'go'! Most of the time however we are unaware of it. Unfortunately our conscious mind and body is rarely able to detect the presence of the life force within us. This is probably due to our conditioning: our minds have been programmed by societies norms. Young children are less distanced from it, but most of us have been brought up not to believe in the power of our own inner healing but in the power of medicine. Rarely have we been encouraged to develop our healing or other psychic senses. More likely it's been suppressed. Thus our conscious mind denies these abilities and doesn't know how to access them. This is where Reiki, or any other form of healer training, comes in. It enables us to sense and connect to the life-force within us, to access the energy as and when we need it.

The role of a 'therapist', the person giving Reiki, is thus to raise our level of awareness of something we already have. Yes, this is a channelling of energy. Not from me to you but between our conscious mind-body and our spiritual, energetic self. It is not a physical channel but a channel between levels of being, between the physical world and higher dimensions. A (Reiki) treatment connects us to our higher self.

The Mind as a Channel

It has been suggested that we, human beings, are using our minds wrongly. Instead of treating them as computers, storing and processing information, we should be using them as communication channels - between our higher self, the universe, and this 3D world of matter. No more, no less. If this is true, then all thoughts, all memories are unnecessary. In fact they are *preventing* us from using our brains properly! To be true channels our minds need to be clear of personal and societal inventions. We don't actually *need* to store memories and ideas! To do so is to clutter up our most precious and valuable sensory organ. It's like having blocked ears or wearing dark glasses . . . we don't see reality. This is probably what the Buddhist approach to enlightenment is about . . . accepting that our mind is not a separate entity but part of the 'Web of Life' (as Fritjof Capra calls it). When we are able to set aside our (selfish) thoughts and (personal) memories so we become open to the vibrations of life, to *all*.

As we discuss in Chapter 25, it is this channel that 'gives' us our psychic abilities. It is our connection to higher realms and, as such, enables us to access information from other times and places. That however is the stuff of Reiki II. For now, let us consider the channel as a conduit for healing energy. A way of manifesting a deep sense of peace and well-being into the body we are physically treating. The energy is already there, but not in this three dimensional world - until we focus our attention on that intent.

Channelling

The world of
spirit & energy

The world of
facts & matter

Make me a channel of thy peace

Channelled Books

A peculiar phenomena of recent years has been the large number of books 'channelled' through to us from another planetary system, galaxy or being (celestial or otherwise). Do libraries class them as 'fact' or fiction'? As we discussed in Chapter 4 the distinction is very blurred. So what are we to make of them? There are No Rules!

Reading channelled books goes well with learning Reiki, but we need to be aware of a number of factors:

* 'Author' - how does the person who put the channelled information down in writing describe themselves: 'channelled by', 'compiled by' or what? I've even seen 'transleated by'!

* 'Author input' - to what extent is the writer adding their own interpretations to what they present as channelled information? Often there is more 'comment' than actual channelled material. We are thus being given this person's personal views and not 'received wisdom'.

* 'The Source' - who, what and/or where are the messages reported as originating? As was discussed above, we cannot expect absolute truth from a source that represents only a single entity, no matter how evolved in might be.

These views from other worlds are often extremely interesting and contain many valuable ideas. They are designed to make us think. Good! We need that. The 'out of this world' perspective presented by channelled books is helpful in getting us to accept that there *are* other life-forms around and they may well be equal or greater in intelligence than us - or of a totally different sort of intelligence.

This is perhaps the most useful role of this genre of book - to help us step out of our notion that having two arms, two legs and a brain makes us civilised and developed. It does nothing of the sort! We are but one form of intelligent life of many. Ours is but one form of consciousness. Books such as 'The Only Planet of Choice' and 'Winds of Change' do much to drag us out of our physical reality. Conscious beings do not have to have physical form. Any devotee of Star Trek knows that!

All too often channelled books spend much time discussing the physical nature of their source. Why? Because it's important? Only to the humans asking questions about the source. Why do we need to attach names and labels to planets we cannot see? We don't. It's all an attempt by our rational minds to control the information, to attach our concepts to new ideas. When are we going to face it - our notion of a universe in three dimensional space is just unreal -

Reiki - Without Rules

or at least extremely limited and limiting. The universe has *many* dimensions. Consciousness extends throughout space, time and at levels few have dreamt of.

Unfortunately (in my humble view) some channelled books, 'The Only Planet of Choice' being a good example, spend far too much of their time giving specifics: names of beings, locations of planets, distinctions between different soul beings. Always labels, theories, models of life. OK, some of this *might* be useful in broadening our perceptions, in helping us to extend our notion of what life is, but there is a danger in all these labels and categories of gods and levels of consciousness - that we might believe them! Does it really matter if there are 7 levels of consciousness and of heaven or 9? Once we've got out of the first 2 or 3 we've left the plane of words anyway!

The enlightenment we seek, the awareness we're developing is beyond beliefs, it doesn't need labels. It just IS.

Does it matter if it was beings from Sirius who came here as Atlanteans . . . or a God who created us in 7 days? Does it? *Really?* However we explain away our existence it is just that, an explanation, a form of words, a model constructed by a human brain or two. The question is whether this model helps us to live our lives. Do any of these theories actually improve our quality of life? Probably not! So why waste time and effort discussing them?

Thus, the channelled books that have had more of an impact on me have been the slimmer ones. The ones with fewer words and fewer 'facts'. Higher wisdom inspires through engaging our higher selves. Books channelled from higher sources and not interfered with are purer, simpler: 'Pathways' by David Knight being a good example. Here we are given an external view of our planet and shown alternative ways of looking at our situation. Simply, without intellectual debate and always with compassion.

The channelled book I particularly recommend however is Beatrice Russell's 'Beyond the Veils'. With only 64 (small) pages it's a slim tome - and all the better for it! It's a collection of channelled meditations, each connecting us to a bit more of our higher self. The idea is that we perform the meditation and experience. By detaching the logical mind we connect to a higher truth. *This* is the way to grow, not by filling our minds with the perceived wisdom of others. *We*, individually, have the answers we need. Follow the lead of the great Frank Sinatra - do it *Your Way*! This is where Reiki comes in - it helps us to become our own channels to the truth.

Some books (channelled or otherwise) can help us see our truth. But how can we become more discerning and only spend time with the books (teachers, etc) that do actually take us *towards* freedom and peace? There are no rules, but the following clues may help:

* The headache. If, when reading something, your head becomes muzzy, then your mind is probably struggling with whatever it's picking up. There could be one of two reasons for this:

* A new challenge. Any new idea could make the brain hurt. Opening up our minds to a wider view of reality is likely to get the brain buzzing a bit!

* A 'stop message'. When we start doing something that is against our best, inner, interests, then our inner self will make this known. It will make life difficult for us; for example by giving us a muzzy head.

So, how to tell the difference? Is the fact that our mind is 'occupied' a sign that it's integrating some new and necessary wisdom, or is it just trying to tell us that what we're trying to assimilate isn't good for us?

To answer this, we need to take a higher perspective, to ask our inner self. The most useful response to a head that's swirling is to lie down. Make time and space to allow the conscious mind to connect to it's higher wisdom. A good time for a self Reiki treatment! Focus on the physical treatment (and/or the symbols). Allow the mind to put whatever caused the muzzy head into perspective. Listen and watch for a sign as to where to go.

Perhaps a light suddenly goes on. Another piece of the jigsaw has fitted into place and our life does make a bit more sense. The new information, the idea from your book for example, is truth. It fits.

Focus on it and let it work it's way through your old ideas, renewing, updating, growing.

Or perhaps you feel angry. Who with? Why? We'll look at anger elsewhere in this book, but for now, be aware that this is a clue to the truth. Maybe you KNOW that what you're reading just isn't true for you - or at least not relevant for you here and now. Listen to this thought. Is *IT* true? It might be the old you not wanting to face the new higher truth. Listen for the deepest, highest voice. *Sense* when your thought is true and act on it. Even gurus get it wrong. Even evolved channelled beings might not understand *your* needs here and now.

Love yourself enough to know your own truth

Now *that* is a channelled truth! It was given to me during a channelling that a friend once offered to do for me. It was about the only sentence of truth from over an hour's communication. The rest was deep anger surfacing from within the channel, re-iteration of various theories, etc, etc. It took all my Reiki experience and focus to distinguish the source and significance of the mixture of messages I was receiving - so it is when reading a book, or listening to a teacher. We each know our own truth - often more clearly than anybody else.

Channelled Art

The truly inspired artists in any art form, be they writer, painter, sculptor, could be considered as being channels to the divine source of all beauty. Is that not what makes the great artists so genuine and their work so powerful? If a clear channel works for them, why not for us!

10 - Hands-on healing

Reiki at First Degree is about 'Hands-On' healing. i.e. the use of physical contact to enable the flow of healing energy. But what exactly does this entail? *Whatever is appropriate!*

Let's first look at this logically. A glance at two or three of the many books now available on the practice of Reiki will show two or three (or more!) possible sets of hand positions for giving a Reiki treatment. All of which will work. So how can one position be 'better' or 'more right' than another? It can't. The right place to put your hands will depend on who's treating who and when.

Luckily Reiki puts us in touch with our intuition and it is this, not some set of printed notes, that provides the best guide as to where and how to place hands during a Reiki treatment.

So why are 'standard positions' so often given? A good question! Maybe because we are so unused to relying on our intuition. Maybe because our habit is to want to be told how to do things rather than encouraged to work things out for ourselves. But times are a changing. And the ability to cope with change is something we are increasingly recognising as being necessary for our survival. Flexibility is what's required in the 21st century. The ability to make our own decisions, to *know* what's best without having to rely on some teacher . . . no matter how well known a guru they may be. Where better to start this process of taking control of our lives than when giving a Reiki treatment.

OK, some guidance would be useful. As we start anything new it's always helpful to hear how others do it and to get some feel for what sort of things tend to work and what doesn't. So, some *guides* to Hands-On Reiki Healing. There are no *rules*. Read the following and be aware of the issues they are raising . . . then do whatever feels right for you.

Hands on or above?

Must the 'giving' hands always be in contact with the 'receiving' body? *Of course not!* In general Reiki healers will place their hands physically on the body they are treating, but on some occasions they may be raised slightly above. This might be appropriate, for example, when:

* The 'receiver' doesn't like having that part of the body touched (e.g. they have ticklish feet or don't like anybody touching the top of their head).

* The 'giver' has a tremble in the 'giving' hand. This might be off-putting to the receiver. Such a tremble can sometimes occur when the amount of energy flowing is high and/or if the 'giving' hand can't be physically supported.

* To focus the energy over a wider area: although Reiki will always go where it needs to, direct contact in a certain place often concentrates the energy at that point . . . sometimes a broader spread may be more appropriate. Others might interpret this situation as 'putting the Reiki into the aura', i.e. healing the etheric or astral body rather than the physical one.

* It feels appropriate to do so! If you need an explanation, choose whichever one of the above seems to fit the treatment in progress.

It is also worth mentioning at this point that Spiritual Healers tend to heal with hands just off the client. In fact this is often the only perceivable difference between a Reiki and Spiritual healing.

To me, the touch that accompanies a Reiki treatment is, in itself, an important feature. Touch is so under used in most western cultures yet is so much part of our bodies need. Enjoy it!

Chakras or Meridians?

Should the hands be placed over chakras or meridians (as used for Shiatsu, Acupuncture, etc)? *Either, neither or both!* Reiki works perfectly well with either the Chakra energy system or the system of meridians . . . but actually requires neither. Thus, you do not need to learn about chakras or meridians in order to do Reiki.

At this stage it is worth pointing out that a Reiki healer does not normally make any form of diagnosis as to their client's conditions. They are not trained to do so. If a Reiki Therapist *does* give a diagnosis, this will almost certainly come from some other discipline where they *are* trained to diagnose. Reiki does not require a diagnosis. Reiki itself knows better than any healer what's needed and why. From time to time during Reiki treatments a therapist may however feel it necessary to relate what they're sensing or otherwise comment on the client's condition. This can be for a number of reasons, for example:

* To reassure the client that we know what's wrong with them and thus put them at their ease.

* To provide feedback to the client as to the cause of their condition so that they can help make appropriate changes in their life.

* The therapist likes to understand (intellectually) what's going on. This may (or may not) actually be necessary!

Basically, diagnoses are to satisfy our logical mind. If factual information doesn't come out of a treatment, don't worry about it. You obviously don't need it.

Hands and Feet

For some reason many 'standard' positions for Reiki treatments miss out our extremities. Given the importance of elbows, knees, hands and feet this is surprising. It is often said that knees and feet correspond to our ability to 'move on' in life (walking, making progress in life, etc). To treat them is thus likely to help us 'take the next step' on our path. If you suffer from cold feet (literally and metaphorically) what better than plenty of Reiki treatments.

If the person receiving the treatment has their hands on their torso, then you can place your hands on theirs and treat the hands AND the body . . . at the same time.

Anytime, any place, anywhere

The beauty of Reiki is that a treatment can be given whenever it's needed. If the 'receiver' is already comfortable, then the treatment can be given wherever they are sitting or lying. Why move them?

We are talking here of treatments to friend and family. Reiki as part of our on-going relationships with all those around us. As a part of our day-to-day lives.

This approach is particularly important when using Reiki for self-treatments. If we pigeon-hole it into something we do for 20 minutes after 'Eastenders' then it could well remain a '20 minutes a day practice' or even become a chore. Whilst it can be useful initially to regularly practice giving yourself treatments these are best given when we need them. This *might* be as we get up in the morning, or as we go to bed at night . . . or even whilst watching our favourite soap. Whenever we're sitting or lying, wherever our hands fall, let that be a signal to start giving ourselves a Reiki. By practising in this way, feeling the flow of Reiki becomes associated with everywhere and nowhere in particular. It becomes a natural activity, without restrictions as to where and when it's performed. The general idea is, if you feel a bit down, or it just feels appropriate to give a Reiki . . . *Just Do It!*

Giving Reiki is to spread love and light into the world. The more we give ourselves the calmer we become, the more open and accepting. It is not selfish to continually treat ourselves. On the contrary. How can we help others if we ourselves are struggling? By loving ourselves we *are* loving the world.

But Where DO I put my hands?

To a beginner, all this freedom can be a bit daunting. Until we get comfortable with following our intuition, some general guide as to where to put hands can be helpful. I still use the following positions as a basis for treatments and during training. They are pretty much as I was taught them . . . and they flow naturally down the body:

1   Eyes

2	3rd Eye (Forehead)
3	Chin
4	Back of head
5	Shoulders (Arms *can* be crossed if that's more comfortable)+
6	Under ribs (or heart)
7	Stomach / abdomen
8	Hips
9	Knees
10	Feet
11	Neck/shoulders
12	Shoulder blades (most easily done by giving yourself a hug)+
13	Small of back / kidneys
14	Coccyx
15	Knees
16	Feet

(+ Comments refer to self treatments)

Before too long, spending 3 to 4 minutes in each of these positions will feel restrictive . . . and isn't necessary. The above pattern can gradually be adapted by just doing what feels right. For example, try:

* Spending more time in one or two positions (where you sense a particular *need*) . . . spending less time in less needy positions.

* Moving the hands from the set position. What do we mean by 'hips' or 'shoulders' anyway! Each of these terms means something slightly different to most of us anyway. Move the hands until they are comfortable for you . . . and right for that particular treatment.

Reiki - Without Rules

Eventually you will find that a treatment is 'free form', hands moving naturally from one position to another, as appropriate to that person at that time. Treating without music assists this process since you won't be tying yourself to a standard timed position. Besides, who wants to be governed by the clock all the time? Reiki is about freeing ourselves from imposed timing constraints and learning to 'go with the flow'. Try taking your watch off before doing Reiki. If you need to be somewhere at a given time, the treatment will end itself in time.

Practical Tips

If you're tired of having to get into impossible positions to give your Reiki treatments, you might find the following tips of help. Remember, there are no rules!

* If some of the positions for treatment are difficult to reach, e.g. you can't get both hands around the feet, do one side at a time, or use just one hand. Far better than straining yourself.

* Don't worry about twisting the body to reach the parts that both hands can't reach! e.g. just use one hand to get round to the coccyx (for self treatment). Whilst two handed positions help give the sense of balance (left to right) they are not essential in any of the Reiki healing positions.

* You *can* cross your hands. e.g. when treating your own shoulders. Reiki is the Universal energy - it's hardly likely to be effected by crossed hands! Such 'rules' (don't cross arms, ankles, etc.) probably come from considering Reiki as other physical energy flows - it isn't. It's within us already. The free flow of Reiki has more to do with our state of mind than our posture.

* Being comfortable is more important than being precise. If you're relaxed, you'll be enabling the flow of Reiki rather than blocking it. Reiki flows whether we're in a lotus position or curled up in a foetal position, or some position unique to you . . . it doesn't matter.

Reiki - Without Rules

11 - The Reiki Principles

As the story of Usui was researched, it became clear that there was more to Reiki than hands-on healing. Powerful though that is, Usui realised that it often worked predominantly at sub-conscious levels. For healing to be most effective the person seeking healing also needs to enter into the healing process at the conscious level: particularly when it's the thought process itself that's causing their disease.

Usui thus promoted what are known as the Reiki Precepts or 'Principles' of Reiki. In New Age terminology these can be considered as affirmations. Tools to positive thinking to support our inner healing. Statements that encourage our mental processes to work with, rather than against the physical and sub-conscious healing.

Given the Buddhist background to Reiki, these precepts come as no surprise. Although not (as far as we know) taken *directly* from Buddhist teachings, they are very much in keeping with the Buddhist aims to rise above our emotions; to develop a mind which is empty of thought, still. Clear of human 'chatter' . . . and thus able to channel the healing energy and wisdom that *is* Reiki.

But they are not just in tune with Buddhist principles. The Reiki Precepts have a Universal Truth about them. They mirror the wisdom that comes from any or all religions and philosophies, for example the oft quoted Christian Prayer "Oh Lord, grant me the courage to change those things I can change, the tolerance to accept those that I cannot . . . and the wisdom to tell the difference".

One difference is however worth highlighting. The Reiki precepts are a blessing, a call for help . . . with a response. Contrast this to the 10 Commandments "Thou shalt not . . . " An order. Rules. Reiki does not deal in written rules. It tells us what to do, often in no uncertain terms, but only as and when required. Generalised rules

Reiki - Without Rules

are rarely helpful. Words of guidance and encouragement are usually far more supportive to those seeking enlightenment.

So, what are these Precepts or Principles? One translation* of a Usui script runs as follows:

The Secret Method of Inviting Blessings

The Spiritual Medicine of Many Illnesses

Today only, anger not, worry not

Do your work with appreciation

Be kind to people

In the morning and at night hold your hands in prayer, meditate on and chant these words

The Usui Reiki system to improve your mind and spirit

* Provided, with thanks, by Dave King, Canadian Teacher and Practitioner of Traditional Japanese Reiki.

One Western version, out of many, goes:

Just for today I will live in an attitude of gratitude

Just for today I will not worry

Just for today I will not anger

Just for today I will do my work honestly

Just for today I will show love and respect for every living thing

The start is important. "Just for today". No generalised target, no all

Reiki - Without Rules

embracing rule, but a simple intent for the here and now. To set ourselves an aim of never worrying or getting angry is probably to set ourselves an impossible challenge, but 'just for today' we might manage!

The sense of the Japanese original is also important: "be in a state of not-worry" (or "not anger"). The meaning emphasises the use of precepts as self affirmations, not as means of control or instruction to others.

Each of the principles stands alone as a statement of how we intend to approach life. There are, however, many interpretations to them, and different levels at which they can be read and/or applied:

"Just for today I will do my work honestly", for example could mean "I'm going to do a good days work, earn my keep, give value for money, not slack, etc." It could also mean "I am going to be honest and truthful in all I do". Not so much what you do, but the way you do it . . . both being important.

The same principle could also mean "I am going to do a worthwhile job". i.e. I am only going to do work which is right for me, which enables me to be true to my inner self". Reiki often forces us to face the fact that the job we're doing is no longer the job we need to be doing. 2 out of my first 100 or so students left their jobs within a week or so of taking Reiki I. Many others have made some change to their working lives. At the time of my own Reiki Masters, I changed course totally - from working in the Quality Assurance of Electronics . . . to teaching Reiki for a living. I had not been working honestly, my work had not been fulfilling. It certainly is now!

It is a common sense amongst those well on their path to make no distinction between the work, rest and play in their life. For one thing to make this distinction is to make judgements, to label, to categorise, none of which are worthwhile activities. But more importantly, when we are being true to ourselves, when we are doing what we came here to do, then life is enjoyable . . . all aspects of it. It's the difference between a job of work and a true vocation. It is our choice whether we do something (for a living or for 'play') that truly feels right or not. Remember that it is us who choose the size of our mortgage and the cost of our living.

"Just for today I will show respect for every living thing". Some versions of the principles instead include statements about honouring our elders. True, the elders in our society often have much to teach us . . . but not always. We can learn just as much, sometimes more, from a new born babe, or a spider, or a football hooligan. Everybody is doing their best. Who are we to judge others?

What about wasps or locusts or other 'pests'? Again, who are we to judge. Just because we can see no benefit for a given creature doesn't mean it's not worthy of respect!

So should we all become vegetarians if we take up Reiki? Not unless that feels like the right thing for *you* to do. Why should we? We are talking about respect for *all* living things . . . including the plants and trees that provide us with nuts and berries . . . and the land which grows our rice and wheat. Whatever we eat we are 'using' the natural world to satisfy our needs. Why separate out animals? How can we compare the natural intelligence of say a cow with, for example, an apple tree. To provide all that fruit on little more than air and water (OK, with a few minerals) is just as much a miracle of nature and worthy of admiration.

So, the emphasis of this principle is the respect bit. To acknowledge the wonder of all living things and to treat them well. And if we are rearing them to feed ourselves, to do so with consideration for their needs . . . in life and in death.

"Just for today I will not worry". We have to admit that we waste a tremendous amount of time feeling anxious or nervous. Time spent worrying achieves nothing. The cause of worry is fear and as Susan Jeffers says (in 'Feel the Fear and Do it Anyway') there is nothing to fear but fear itself. The idea of this principle is to recognise when we are feeling worried and to face the fear. Feelings of fear result from an unrealistic view of a situation. When we *do* face it we'll nearly always find that even if the worse happens we'll be fine. Besides, who are we to label a particular outcome 'best' or 'worse'? With

Reiki comes faith. If the Universe is asking us to do something, then it will support us in that endeavour. As we learn to trust the Universe, so we learn that it *does* care for us.

The other side of this is that sometimes feelings of anxiety come when we *know* we shouldn't be doing something. A nervous sensation results when our inner self and conscious mind see things differently. Say we *want* to go on a particular date. We feel anxious. Maybe this is because there's so much to be gained from it . . . and thus so much (in our ego human conscious mind) to be lost by not doing it. Or maybe our inner self knows that this relationship isn't right for us. Maybe we *know* that it will only result in the same old problems as the last one. In this case, by facing those fears we begin to see, perhaps, how our conditioning attracts us to 'the wrong men' or 'the wrong women' (for us): i.e. a certain type of man or woman with whom we're bound to have a co-dependent and unhealthy relationship.

Look further into these feeling and the real issues begin to come out, and we can move forward in our relationships and in our lives. By not allowing ourselves to dwell on worry, but instead facing it, we might find, for example, that the folks we're attracted to remind us very much of our parents. It could be that many of the feeling we experience are really feelings for our father or mother . . . and it is perhaps these that need to be acted upon . . . not our apparent attraction!

Feelings are often not what they seem. They are often indicators of a deeper issue . . . and are our inner self's way of saying 'Hey! isn't it time you dealt with this?!" Thus, when the principles say "do not worry" or "do not anger" they are certainly not saying suppress those emotions. On the contrary, they are saying face them. Deal with them. Don't let old emotions rule your life!

It's worth making a distinction perhaps two sorts of emotion:

First we have a genuine 'here and now' feeling - where we respond naturally to a particular situation and allow ourselves to express whatever sensations comes to us or over us. Having expressed it (e.g. crying with grief when someone close dies, sharing in the joy of a compatriots gold medal, etc.), we move on. No residue. Heart and mind free to respond naturally to the next moving situation.

Secondly we have a conditioned reaction. A stored emotion, where it's not the here and now situations that induces our expression of sadness, anger (or whatever) but something deeper. We often react to situations that trigger repressed emotions. If we haven't grieved fully for a loved one, then any death or funeral will trigger that grief.

As we use Reiki in our lives and become aware of our emotions, so we see patterns. We begin to realise where we are being true to a situation and where we are merely repeating old patterns or reacting through past memories. By giving ourselves Reiki treatments we help the past to come to the surface and thus live more naturally here and now.

"Just for today I will not anger". If something or somebody makes us angry the chances are that they are triggering an issue we are not at peace with. Nobody *makes* us angry. Anger is of our own making. Even if somebody has set out to annoy you, you don't have to rise to the bait. When we have peace of mind, when our conscious mind is in tune with our inner self, then we *are* calm. Anger is an indication that we are not at peace with ourselves. Again the only realistic approach is to face that anger, to ask what *exactly* it is that you're angry about.

Say, for example, your neighbour is always parking in front of your house. You don't have a car, so don't need the space yourself but it annoys you. Why? Maybe you think he's being selfish? Umm! By projecting such an accusation onto others, the chances are that it applies to us. The anger might just be jealousy that your neighbour *has* a car! Perhaps you're not as happy with being car-less as you thought?

"Just for today I will live in an Attitude of Gratitude" or 'Count your many blessings' as other religions might say. The Universe provides for all our needs - not our wants, our genuine needs. By acknowledging this and thanking God for providing for us, we are consciously accepting the unique relationship between ourselves and the Universe.

At the day to day level, it's about thanking others for their help, about making compliments when they're deserved, about finding positive things to say . . . instead of criticising and moaning all the time. As we give so we receive. If we want others to compliment and thank us, then the best start is to set an example . . . and mean it.

There is another way of looking at this principle: everything that happens has meaning. Everybody we meet has something to teach us. Even 'bad' things have a positive message. Once we accept this about life, so we rise above the need to label events 'good' or 'bad'. Everything *is*.

"Just for today I . . . " don't restrict yourself to the 6 oft quoted principles. Try adding a few of your own. Make up a new one from time to time to suit your mood, to help you cope with whatever's giving you trouble at that time. There was a period, for example, when I found myself judging others all the time "he's too competitive", "she's fat", etc. Not a very enlightened thing to do! I needed to accept others as they are. I thus found it useful to focus on a principle of my own: "Just for today I will not judge". Whenever I found myself making snap decisions about folks I would say this a few times. And then perhaps another affirmation: "I accept everything and everybody as they are now, ever have been and ever will be". With this approach to life, far less is going to bother us.

64

12 - The Aspects of Reiki

Reiki works at many different levels, often at the same time. It can also work predominantly at say the physical level for one person on one occasion but on a different level for the same person on another occasion. Reiki works at the level in needs to work. But what's meant by 'level'? A useful description comes from a consideration of the Four Aspects of Reiki:

Aspects of Reiki

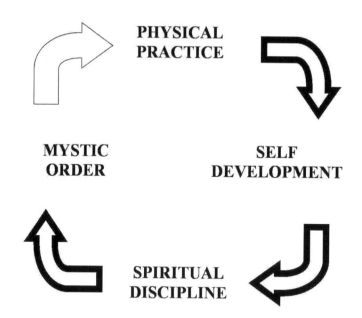

PHYSICAL PRACTICE

SELF DEVELOPMENT

SPIRITUAL DISCIPLINE

MYSTIC ORDER

This idea was presented by Phyllis Lei Furumoto (Lineage Bearer)

Reiki - Without Rules

at the Reiki Gathering in Cork, Ireland in 1996. Although based on her definitions, the descriptions given here result from my own experiences.

Physical Practice

Reiki starts for many people as a physical treatment, a simple hands-on healing aimed at easing tension and bringing about a relaxed state. The treatment and effects are predominantly physical. At this level, Reiki is a practice, something we set time aside for and do as a separate activity.

The second meaning of 'practice' is also important: as we give and/or receive more Reiki so we become more practised in allowing it to do what it needs to. Our minds and bodies become open to the Reiki and we find ourselves getting more from a treatment. The Reiki itself, through practice, is helping us to accept it as rather more than a physical practice!

Self Development

It is now widely accepted that most, if not all, physical conditions have a corresponding emotional and/or mental aspect. 'As above, so below'. Thus, physical dis-ease is often the result of a mental conflict. Help the mind to find peace and as our head clears so do bodily symptoms. Conversely, by helping the body to relax (as during a Reiki treatment) we allow our minds to unwind.

The second aspect of Reiki thus recognises the mind:body link in terms of our physical health and mental well-being. Through regular physical practice of Reiki we help ourselves to develop as human beings. Reiki IS a self-development method - particularly at Reiki II (Second degree), where we can use the symbols to help us face and deal with bad habits and mental blocks.

Spiritual Discipline

As we work with Reiki and allow it to relax us totally in mind and body, so we begin to connect with our true, inner, higher, self. Here we see Reiki as an holistic practice. We begin to see that the 'problems' in our life arise out of a denial of our spiritual self. Through Reiki we (re)learn to listen not just to our bodies but to our souls. Reiki helps us to see that the sense of fulfilment that we seek in life comes not from material 'haves' but from 'being' true to our inner selves . . . AND it gives us a means of connecting to that part of us. Reiki practice is akin to meditation and prayer.

I use the word 'practice' many, many(!), times in this chapter for reason and effect. My thesaurus gives me no alternative:

* 'Routine' suggests doing the same time and time again - but every time we do Reiki it's different. There is nothing routine about the practice of Reiki!

* 'Exercise' again suggests 'going through the motions' and/or a physical thing. A Reiki treatment (or 'session') is not a physical exercise - unless it's an exercise in allowing our soul to guide us.

* 'Habit'? Well maybe! Certainly we get the most from Reiki when it becomes second nature to us, habitual. But on an 'as and when required' basis, not a 'third Friday of the month' basis.

So the idea is to become accustomed to the flow of Reiki, to allow it to guide us. To *begin with* it might be useful to have a set routine to and for your Reiki sessions, but flexibility is important. The more *self* disciplined we are, in following only the path of higher truth, the more 'connected' and 'real' we feel.

Mystic Order

A mystic order experience cannot be described in words. It is beyond words. But in a book, words are all we have. So it is, perhaps, that sense of being 'everywhere and nowhere', a feeling of being totally at peace with the world. It is about being IN the here and now . . totally aware of where you are, yet *through* that moment being 'as One with God'. Mystic Order experiences rarely come through trying . . . they just happen. This can be whilst watching a sunset, making love, *in* a dance . . . or during a Reiki treatment or attunement.

Immersion

Because a Mystic Order experience is beyond words, is it difficult to portray it. It is not some philosophical concept but a sensation embracing *all* our senses and indeed our very sense of being. We feel *immersed* in life itself. And that is not such a strange idea. What happens when we become engrossed in an activity which we feel is 'us'? We become immersed in it. It 'takes us over', there is no distinction between us (our mind and body) and that which we are doing . . . be it baking a cake, painting a landscape, dancing, fixing our car . . . whatever. A mystic order experience is accessible to anyone. It does not require any particular technique. Many natural, down to earth people enjoy life. They just get on with what they have to do, throw themselves into it mind, body and soul. Few will have any philosophical words to describe what they're doing - they're just living as best they're able - fully, with total absorption in life itself. Free from doubts and worries: for their mind is always focused on the job in hand . . . whatever it might be: driving a rally car, the 100m at the Olympics, tending a vegetable garden. When we live totally in the here and now, when our mind has no other thoughts, *that* is truly living . . . the mystic order to being human.

The whole idea is a balance between the mystical, the magical and the structured, the ordered. The idea of Divine Order, chaotic but with a purpose . . . although probably not one accessible to human minds.

Thus our spiritual discipline helps us to surrender to the Divine Order, to take our true place in the natural order of things. To BE who we are meant to be. As Reiki becomes not so much of a practice but a way of life, so mystic order experiences happen more frequently and more easily. Gradually we find that we can BE, not just in magical places but anywhere and everywhere. Reiki helps us to live as the spiritual beings we are actually *in* the everyday world.

68

Self Supporting

In reality, these four aspects cannot be separated. We *are* mind, body and soul. Each Reiki treatment is a step in our personal growth, each ache and pain a reflection of a denial or healing process in the mind. For those not yet comfortable with the idea of being 'beings of light', using Reiki to help with relaxation will do the trick, and help prepare us for . . . whatever we need. The more we practice, the greater progress we'll make on our developmental path and the closer we'll get to truly mystical experiences . . . and the more we'll *want* to practice.

And so the cycle continues. Each mystic order experience encourages us to practice more - which untangles a few more mental blocks which helps us be even more true to the Divine within us. We begin to accept our responsibility for our Quality of Life and to 'lighten up'. We have the energy to create our heaven on earth . . . and the wisdom to know when to use it!

Meditation

If Reiki can be considered a spiritual practice, how does it relate to meditation? That depends what you mean by meditation! Depending on your school of thought, meditation can mean all sorts of things to all sorts of people. More often than not we get an image of sitting cross legged in silence (or perhaps chanting a mantra) with incense burning. Either our eyes are closed or we have a candle lit, giving ourselves a focus for our attention.

Such is the conventional view of meditation which undoubtedly gives a great deal of satisfaction to many people. But by no means to all. The physical discipline, considered an essential part of it to some, to others gets in the way. After all, why should we have to be uncomfortable to meditate? We don't.

The Chambers English Dictionary gives as a definition: *"Meditate: to consider thoughtfully: to engage in contemplation: to consider deeply, reflect upon: to revolve in the mind: to intend."*

It is the last of these that rings most true with me. If our intent is to connect to our higher self, to find that still, peaceful, wise, place within us, then we are on the meditation path. When we succeed in finding that 'place' then we are, to my way of thinking, meditating.

As to how we achieve this, that's up to each of us. *There are no rules*. Walking meditations or those assisted by improvised singing or playing of a musical instrument come out high on the list of effective methods - because they emphasise individuality and a *living* peace. We don't have to be physically still or silent to meditate! Thus doing a Reiki treatment is, to many, a sort of meditation. Meditation and Reiki healing are mutually supportive.

Reiki - Without Rules

13 - Intent

What is your intent in taking up Reiki Healing? Do you want to help your friends and family? Do you realise that you've lost you path in life and want to regain it? Or do you just know you *have* to do it? *There are no rules.* Whatever guides you into Reiki is right for you but, if anything, the last reason is the best. If you're doing something because you just *have* to, then you're already listening to your inner voice. In Reiki we need no better reason to do something than because we *know* it's the right thing to do. Our higher self usually knows far better than our rational self as to what's in our best interest . . . and thus in everybody else's.

For the Greater Good

The issue of intent is particularly important when we are treating other people. *Why* are we treating them? *Because it's the right thing to do at that time.* If we give treatments because we're pressured into it or feel obliged to, then it may be that it's not really appropriate . . . in such cases we'd probably find not much happened anyway.

Before giving any treatment we usually take a few moments to focus ourselves, to clear our minds ready for the job in hand (so to speak). It is important at this point to free ourselves from any preconceived ideas as to the outcome of the treatment. One way to do this is to state (to ourselves) our intent. For example "I intend to be a healing channel for the greater good", or "I channel love and light into this person. May God's will be done". It is not for us, as mere channels for the energy, to attempt to influence the outcome. We are not the healers, merely the instrument of healing. Reiki is the ultimate wisdom and knows what needs to happen. Our healing treatment merely helps the natural process along.

Dying Peacefully

A particular instance of this approach is when dealing with those who are terminally ill. We might *want* to cure them, we might have been asked to "make them well", but it is not for us to take on such a task. True, healing *can* be miraculous. Major diseases *can* be turned around with Reiki or other therapies. But to *expect* such a result is unwise . . in that any expectation is to suggest that we know best. We don't.

A more usual scenario is that Reiki given to those close to dying can assist the parting. It can ease the transition from this world to the next. It can greatly assist dying to be a natural, peaceful, process. Just as importantly, Reiki given to those close to the person dying can help them to accept what is happening. Dying, to those who live Reiki, is merely a change in level of existence, it's no big deal. Reiki treatments can thus be used to break down some of the taboos which surround death and to help us face the associated fears.

Through Reiki we can find a place of beauty and peace . . . where it doesn't matter what happens next . . . in life or death.

Intent is All

It is often said in Reiki that the intent in a treatment or training session is all. By this we mean that when we set our intent as the channelling of healing, then the healing will occur - as and when it needs to. The intent is far more important than the hand positions adopted, what sort of music is played, length of treatment, or any other practical considerations. It's worth remembering this when doing a treatment: if nothing seems to be happening *Don't Panic!* Instead of worrying if the hands are in the wrong place, focus on your intent. You are giving love to this person. That is what a Reiki treatment amounts to, and that is what matters most during a treatment.

Intent for Whom?

This does raise the question as to who this intent is aimed at, who benefits from it? It could certainly be argued that our intent has no impact on the Reiki healing energy or thus on the treatment - we have little if any influence over the Universal energy! Thus, the healing will continue anyway and the 'client' will receive the healing they need - pretty much whatever we do.

The intent is primarily for our own benefit. To focus our mind and attention, to help us be with the treatment - in mind, body and soul. The more 'with it' we are, the more relaxed we'll be. This has a number of benefits:

* The client will sense that we are relaxed and that will help them to relax also.

* We'll be more receptive to the Reiki flow and get the healing *we need.*

* With both parties relaxed, a resonance will build up and the flow of Reiki will probably be greater.

Our intent is thus a statement of our commitment to the treatment. We are telling the Universe, and ourselves, that it's the greater good that matters most to us.

14 - Attunements

One of the few differences between Reiki Healing and other forms of healing is that Reiki training includes what are known as attunements. The idea is that during this process the student is literally 'tuned into' the Reiki energy - as a radio might be tuned into BBC World Service. i.e. the ability of the student to act as a channel for Reiki energy is enhanced.

The process is also sometimes called an initiation. i.e. the student is 'initiated into Reiki', or at second degree 'initiated into the Reiki symbols'. This process, by whatever name, is often quite a complex ritual, a series of special treatments by the attuning Reiki Master using particular combinations of symbols and positions. It is indeed a sacred process. Perhaps the first time a student has felt such a powerful connection to the God within them. It is perhaps similar to a blessing given by holy men or women from other traditions. In giving attunements I often feel that I am giving a blessing . . . although occasionally it feel as though I am receiving one . . . and a wonderful experience it is!

There is some debate as to how much of the ritual and procedure is actually necessary. Much is included perhaps to emphasise the sacred nature of the event. However, when attunements of a number of Masters are compared, the differences are often significant . . . yet the end result (students who are now in tune with the Reiki within them) is the same.

As with treatments, each person undergoing an attunement experiences something unique to them. Whilst colours and floating sensations are quite common, there is no one experience associated with any particular attunement. Some will feel very little, some will experience a state of bliss that is indescribable. As with treatments we each get what we need at that time. The effect of an attunement could well relate to how aware of the energy we are before we take it. Those with existing psychic abilities or who have done much self development work are far more likely to experience the more profound pleasures than those new to the mystical side of life . . but there are no rules.

My own experience suggests that each attunement opens up the channel (as described in Chapter 9) a bit more: starting from wherever that person happens to be. There are no absolutes in Reiki. One First Degree student may have had hundreds of Mystic Order experiences before, another none. An attunement is hardly likely to have the same effect on both of them.

Sometimes a treatment may have the effect of an attunement . . . particularly if it's the first ever Reiki treatment. After all, doesn't 'initiation' mean 'the first time'? The line between treatment and attunement is perhaps not as significant as some would make out. Or perhaps it's a matter of intent . . . not so much on the part of the teacher but of the student: if they take a treatment with the intent of finding out what Reiki is like and possibly taking it up, then that treatment will effectively be an initiation. If, however, another student goes to a Reiki I class with the intent of having a relaxing weekend, then their attunement may have the relaxing effect of a treatment and no more. The Reiki will provide whatever is needed to the student . . . and to the Master teacher.

But what IS an attunement?

The best way to find out, is to experience one. But don't go with any particular expectations, or you're likely to be disappointed.

During an attunement you are enabled to connect between your conscious mind:body and you higher, spiritual, self. During the process you are opened up to this higher level of consciousness . . . and an ability to connect at this new higher level will remain with you after the session.

Words do not do the process justice. Whilst some students are just relaxed by an attunement it is not unusual for a attunement to literally take somebody 'out of themselves'. It can be a powerful, even profound, experience. One which can leave you feeling lightheaded and/or 'not quite with it'. Which isn't surprising, since we are opening up to parts of ourselves which have been lost to us, probably since birth. The sensation, and resulting re-adjustment in our mind's working, can take some time to work through. It's important to give yourself this time, probably alone, to assimilate each attunement. This is one reason why I usually run First Degree Reiki over a weekend (including Friday night) or 3 days, to allow more time for students to soak up the attunement experience.

If you've had an attunement and felt nothing of this, don't worry. It *may* be that the attuning Master wasn't sufficiently attuned themselves, or in-tune with you. Or it could be that you were not ready for any major experience. Either way, the experience *was* what you needed at that time. Quite likely you'll be led to another course, maybe a different Master, to take it up again at a later date . . . or guided onto a path other than Reiki.

Cumulative Effect

The effect of attunements can be heightened by any of the following factors:

* Length of time the Master is with each student: this allows for a greater focus of the energy to each individual. It becomes more personal and thus more effective.

* Number of attunements: at First Degree most Masters do 4 separate attunements within the course. Each one will 'build on' the effects of the previous one. It's not unusual for the first one or two to have little effect but for the third or fourth to be really felt.

* Number of students being attuned at the same time: An amplification effect seems to come into play. In a large class, less time with each student is more than balanced by this group effect.

* Experience of the initiating Master - not just in doing attunements but in terms of general level of awareness and progress on their path to enlightenment. There are no absolutes in who can become a Master, so you may need to 'shop around' to find one who *does* exude the truth and light that you feel drawn to.

Transition

The ritual within many cultures can be a necessary part of some key events in life. In particular, having a set framework within which to operate can help us through a difficult time. Thus rituals are traditionally part of major transitions in our lives: marriage, death, etc. It is suggested by Robert Bly in 'Iron John', for example, that the lack of ritual for 'coming of age' has created major problems in many cultures. By not passing through some initiation ceremony, girls and boys do not acknowledge or perhaps even complete their move into adulthood.

Thus the ceremony and ritual of a Reiki attunement is an important part. It helps us acknowledge the significance of the moment.

Too much ritual can get in the way, it can detract from what's actually happening. Too little, however, and the importance of the moment can be lost and students may not fully appreciate or experience what's happening to them. Some ritual helps to focus our attention on the here and now, to be part of the process. Within Reiki attunements the holding of a student's hands by the Master emphasises the connection between them, helping to show that this is a personal experience. T*his* student, *now*, is undergoing a transition to a higher state of consciousness.

This is probably a good time to mention Absent Attunements. Giving an attunement 'at a distance' is definitely possible and likely to be effective. How can it not be? However, without a ritual and personal element to it, there is a risk that the student will not fully participate in the process and thus may not get the full benefit. In emphasising that there are no rules, we *do* need to be aware of the issues involved in choosing a given way of working.

Too Much?

Since Reiki is self regulating, it's unlikely we can over-do attunements. However, too many attunements in rapid succession can trigger a major healing crisis, or open up more than we feel ready to cope with. Be wary of cramming too many training sessions or attunements into a short space of time. Give each one time to 'sink in' before moving on to higher levels of Reiki or different energy systems. You can't hurry love . . . nor the process of becoming a true channel for it.

At the other extreme, many of us are fairly blocked to our higher selves and need quite a 'zap' to open up that channel. This is probably why four attunements are deemed necessary at First Degree.

So, if you're concerned about having too many, or too few, attunements, or of moving on 'too quickly', just relax! Give yourself a treatment and listen to your inner self. If the thought of more Reiki training makes you nervous, then your body is telling you to look more closely at this next step. Is it an excited nervousness? The adrenaline flowing to prepare you for a new, if challenging, adventure? If so, this is something you HAVE to do - so book that course now! Or, is your intuition warning you that you're NOT ready? Only *you* know what you need at any given moment - so ask yourself.

The conclusion, as always, is that *there are no rules*. We each take the path that seems right for us. Both within and between Reiki training courses an aware Master will sense when each student has 'had enough' (or needs more) and will act accordingly. All you have to do is enter into the spirit of it . . . and enjoy.

Reiki - Without Rules

15 - The Effects

What we feel during and after a healing treatment will depend on many things. We will feel different things at different times and when treated by different people. Some will experience all sorts of wonderful sensations, others hardly anything. Why such a wide variation? *Because we are all different, with different needs and different abilities.* We experience what we need to experience at that particular moment.

Healing Crisis

Things often get worse before they get better. In this respect Reiki Healing is no different to other Complementary Therapies. It is rarely 'a quick fix'. Reiki treatments dislodge physical blockages and release toxins. These need to work through the system, which can take some time. Some report a '21 day healing cycle', although it is unclear where the figure of 21 days comes from. Many people will feel no negative after-affects from a treatment, some will find it triggers a significant bout of cold or flu type symptoms. This *might* last a few days or weeks. Or you might find that once you start doing Reiki on yourself that, as one thing after another is faced and released, you have a series of 'colds' or various aches and pains. The best advice is usually to recognise when this is happening and give yourself time and space to let the healing process work itself through.

Two particular physical effects which may accompany a healing crisis are worthy of mention:

* A fever - sometimes, when the energy is really flowing, we may feel feverish, alternating hot and cold. A sure sign that the Reiki is shifting physical and emotion baggage. Usually we have no choice but to curl up somewhere warm and quiet and let it take its course - if we fight it, we'll only feel worse.

* Painful tears - whilst crying is a frequent effect of Reiki, as long held emotions are finally released, from time to time we may experience something more than a moistening of the eyes or tears streaming down our face. Occasionally my tears have really stung my eyes. It's as if the tears contain so much toxic material that they are harmful. Such tears may only last a few minutes and the stinging goes once the eyes are washed out. The feeling of release at such time is wonderful. There goes some *really* deep seated bad habits!

Engaged

You may feel that for some time during and/or after a treatment that your mind feels busy, as if you're getting an 'engaged' tone. This is pretty much what is happening! A (Reiki) healing experience can be profound. Reiki training can challenge our whole view of life. Not surprisingly our minds need time and space to absorb the experience, to let the energy work though whatever healing process it started. This could be a major 'rewiring' exercise and is quite likely to fully occupy the mind for anything from a few seconds to many years. During this time we won't want to be bothered with much at all. Little will hold our attention. We'll want to detach ourselves from life. Which is exactly what we need to do. Take a few steps back and see our life as if from outside. See with refreshed eyes and a clearer mind who and what we are and where we're going in life. If we need to be left alone to deal with it, the Universe will give us that time and space.

Any particular ache or pain is likely to be an indicator of a held-in condition. Perhaps aching shoulders indicting that we're shouldering too many responsibilities. In 'Reiki - Universal Life Energy' Bodo Baginski gives a useful correlation between symptoms and emotional or life situations. Not to be taken literally all the time, but often a useful guide. Louise Hay ("You Can Heal Your Life", etc.) was one of the first to write about this correspondence between physical dis-ease and the aspects of our lives and attitudes that often cause it. Well worth reading and reflecting on.

So, it's a good idea to place our hands on wherever is aching and allow our minds to reflect on the corresponding issue. Let the energy flow from hands to position and to the part of the brain dealing with the related topic. If you have 2nd degree, throw the symbols at any picture that comes to mind. Feel the heat at the contact point burning away any blockages. Perhaps it relates to a condition you've had since childhood . . . the more years you've had the condition the longer it's likely to take to bring the real issue to the surface and to reprogram the mind. Memories are locked in our cells, so we need to treat them as well as the brain and mental processes.

Chilli Beans

Maybe you feel a hot spot in the brain - like a chilli bean. I find it useful to focus attention on this spot . . . it might get so hot it's almost unbearable, but go with it. Visualise the energy zapping away at this part of the brain. Perhaps it's literally a mental block. An area where thoughts go round and round in circles. So imaging the Reiki untangling this mass, clearing the mind of the endless loop and enabling thoughts to pass through this bit of the mind more freely. You may not be aware of what particular thought process or issue it's working on, but from then on, one less thing is going to bother you. Each chilli bean effect is a mental block being dissolved and one less issue in life to get you worked up. I'm afraid you're likely to have many chilli con carnes before your life is free of 'things that get to you', but every little helps.

Tinnitus

Since I first started 'sorting myself out' (8 years before I took up Reiki) and exploring matters psychic and spiritual, I've 'suffered' from tinnitus. Eventually I noticed that the ringing in the ears varied in intensity and location depending on what sort of thinking I was doing. When I was relaxed and content, with no big issues to concern myself with, I had little if any tinnitus. After a new psychic experience or whilst reading a challenging book, the tinnitus would rise in 'volume'. There was a definite correlation between the extent of the ringing 'in' my ears and the degree to which I was challenging my long held beliefs. I concluded that my tinnitus is literally the sound of my brain working. Since then, with the help of Reiki, I've learnt to recognise the tinnitus as an indicator of my 'state of mind'. Heavy tinnitus means that my brain is 'engaged' on serious reprogramming work - working through some issue and moving forward with its re-alignment (see Chapter 31). Once that issue is cleared, then the tinnitus diminishes.

Those with tinnitus may thus find that the symptom actually gets worse during and/or immediately after a Reiki treatment . . . but that by taking up Reiki and working with it and the tinnitus over a period of months or years, that a time will come when the tinnitus is present less often . . . and even when it's there we'll be able to treat it as a friend.

A taste in the mouth

We all know the expressions about things we find 'difficult to swallow' or that 'leave a nasty taste in the mouth' or which we find 'hard to stomach'. Such situations are often present during a healing crisis. When our aim is to face realities then, quite often, we *will* be trying to swallow some unpleasant facts. E.g. that even our closest friends can't always be trusted to keep their word. The related physical symptoms often accompany such times of acceptance. With apologies to any reader with medical training, my greatly simplified explanation of this would be as follows: mental reprogramming causes significant brain activity which involves chemical action. Toxins too are released in the process. All these chemical are, or result in, the phlegm, mucus, or whatever yuck we sense at the back of our throat.

As with emotions, my experience is that such waste products are 'better out than in'. I often have a dish or mug at my side during such periods, so that I can spit out the yuck. I find that not spitting it out causes coughing and often a churned up feeling in the stomach . . . which isn't surprising, if it *is* toxic waste, our digestive system is likely to react against it! What I've also noticed at such times is that a conscious effort to think positive and not to dwell on the doubts and old thoughts greatly reduces the amount of mucus, etc produced. This would seem to support the theory that the phlegm (etc) results from the mental 'battle' between 'real' and conditioned thoughts. Fuel the battle (by allowing doubts to fester) and the yuck is produced far more than if we surrender gracefully to our higher self.

16 - Practical Aspects

To me, Reiki is something you can do anytime, anyplace, anywhere. This helps it to become part of our day-to-day life. So, no rules. However, there are some pointers that those new to using Reiki . . . and indeed some who've been practising for some time, might find useful. Where you do Reiki is a matter of personal preference and whatever is convenient. I very rarely use a massage couch, preferring a futon mattress on the ground; but that could be because I'm a 'cat person' and prefer to sprawl than to stand! So long as both the person 'giving' and 'receiving' are comfortable, that's all that really matters.

The Sound of Silence

Is background music necessary for Reiki? *Not usually.* On the contrary. Music intended to be in the background is something of nothing. Either you play music with a more positive and helpful purpose or treat in silence. The Sound of Silence, when accompanied by the uplifting effects of Reiki, can leave us refreshed and clear thinking. Why clutter that feeling with unnecessary sound?

Having said that, sometimes music is helpful. For example:

* Where both 'giver' and/or 'receiver' are new to Reiki and worried about not being able to relax into it. This is usually an unreal fear, but if some relaxation type music helps to still the mind, use it.

* Where both parties particularly enjoy music and would like to bring together the musical and Reiki experiences. Music, like Reiki, is an energy. When the two are in harmony the experiences can be greatly heightened: let the healing energy pulse in time with the music, allow the rhythms of the sound to work with the Reiki in our very bodies and souls. My first, and still one of the most memorable, experience of this was treating a lady accompanied by the Brandenberg Concertos. Wow! . . . although words can't really

describe it. There is no "Reiki Music" as such. Any music that feels right for you can be used to accompany a treatment. If you can do it with live music, even better . . . Reiki with Didgeridoo accompaniment is a particular favourite of mine!

* To help in timing a treatment. When starting Reiki it can be useful to spend a few minutes in each of a number of treatment positions, to get used to the act of 'hands-on healing'. To experience the energy flow at different parts of the body is useful in learning the range of sensations we can sense during treatment. A piece of music with a bell every 3 or 4 minutes can help: this is usually what is meant by 'Reiki Music'. However, many such tapes guide you through a particular set of positions explaining what that position 'does'. This can be restrictive. My preference, and what I use in my classes, is a CD with 15 or 16 tracks on. One position per track. When the music changes, you move your hands . . . a sort of musical chairs.

Laugh or Cry

A Reiki treatment is not a serious medical procedure . . . unless you want it to be. Whether giving or receiving, being comfortable is the main thing . . . and let whatever emotions surface come out. It's often useful to have some tissues handy. Reiki can release much that needs to come out of our system. It doesn't have to be tears, laughter is not uncommon. Or maybe what's triggered is an outpouring of thoughts and feelings in words. Whatever, just let it come. Allow the mind to release whatever it has to. It's better out than in.

Alexander Technique

Whether you're standing or kneeling to give a treatment, the strain on your own body can be significant. Whilst the Reiki itself will help to limit any adverse effects, anything we can do to help us get comfortable is going to help. The more relaxed we are, the more relaxed will be the 'client'. One useful technique for adopting a good body posture during Reikis, is the Alexander Technique which I suggest investigating for its own benefits anyway.

I was particularly impressed when I did a weekend course on the Alexander Technique, for one main reason: the philosophy and practice was to *connect* us to the world around us, not to isolate us from 'the outside world'. A typical Alexander Technique relaxation technique, for example, has you laying on your back on the floor, focusing on your breathing. Nothing unusual there, much like other meditation techniques, except that we were told to keep our eyes *open*. Like Reiki, the idea is to be aware of both our own internal needs *and* what's going on around us.

Inner Sights

Using music to assist the Reiki healing is often useful - to help to (re)focus the mind. Another powerful tool is to add visualisations to our self treatments. The aim is to enable our mind to detach itself from day-to-day cares - like what's for dinner! Such written or lead visualisations are meant only as a starting point. Once the mind has got hold of it and entered into the spirit of it, just let it go on its own journey. Allow the imagination to take over, explore the inner recesses of your mind - you never know what's in there just waiting to come out! My "Rosy Tinted Glasses" (see list of books at the back) includes many such guided meditations.

Or the following might, for example, be suitable if doubts are creeping in, or if we're feeling that our light is fading:

Turn up the Gas!

Picture yourself as a light. Imagine what sort of a light you might be . . . a candle, a spot light, a lighthouse? See the light shining out from your inner self, through your mind and body. OK, it's rather dim at present, look for the reason and send in the maintenance crew to fix it. Say you're a gas light and somebody has turned down the gas supply. Picture yourself turning the tap so that more gas flows into your light. The channel for the energy from the Universe to you has been opened wide, you begin to glow brightly. Feel the energy flow, the light shining into you, through you. Perhaps feel it light up your body as it flows through you . . . each vein becoming a fibre-optic, lighting up as the laser light passes down each arm and leg. Gradually the light builds up until your whole body is a wonderful display. Perhaps it's brilliant white, or maybe a kaleidoscope of colour, constantly changing. Or maybe it's brilliant white AND all the colours of the rainbow . . . and a few that haven't been invented yet. Turn on the energy, let the light flow, let your inner self live again!

Sacred Spaces

Doing Reiki in a 'sacred space' can bring an extra dimension to a treatment - but Reiki can be done anywhere. Better perhaps to realise that *all* space is sacred space . . . not just the historical sacred places like stone circles, ruined abbeys or other places that have a cultural significance to you.

Any place of natural beauty is certainly a sacred site, and to do Reiki in a peaceful garden, on a beach, under a ancient tree, etc. can certainly help to feel connected to all that is natural and peaceful. But if this isn't possible, don't worry about it. If you like, you can light candles, burn oils or incense or otherwise turn the room your treating in into a more obviously sacred place . . . *but you don't need to!* Reiki works anytime, any place, any where.

Being in, or creating a sacred place can help 'set the scene' for a Reiki treatment; in the same way as playing music can. Particularly when starting out with Reiki, such details can help . . . but are not necessary. Being surrounded by things with positive, natural, energy will help us to relax and focus on being natural ourselves, but the real source of positive energy is within us - wherever we happen to be. With practice, we'll find that Reiki flows in a crowded underground carriage, in a school classroom . . . anywhere and everywhere.

17 - The $10,000 Question

Money is a fact of modern society. We cannot escape it's influence and rarely can we do without it. But we don't have to let it rule our lives.

Money *is* an issue in Reiki. And rightly so. Our attitude towards financial matters has much to answer for. Wherever we see fear or poverty, oppression or exploitation then money, (or at least 'profit' or 'progress' or 'development') is often behind it. We use it as an excuse for so much. In truth money is a tool. As such it can be used for any purpose; 'good' or 'bad' . . . it's just that we all have different ideas as to what constitutes good and bad . . . and are often prepared to pay dearly for those ideas.

Lets put this into perspective. I write this is on a Psion hand-held computer, sitting in my garden. The Autumn sun is warm on my arms, and the birds are singing. I look up to the neighbour's apple tree and watch a robin singing of the joy of life. A bit further down is a finch . . . I don't normally see one of those here. Wow! I'm waiting for a call back from my bank to confirm an extended overdraft . . . but it doesn't matter! My purse, wallet and larder are almost empty . . . but it doesn't matter . . . I've just picked two meals worth of blackberries from my hedge and all is wonderful.

Money is an energy. We buy electricity and gas with it. We know that by tending our garden with love it rewards us with fruit. We know that when we support our friends and neighbours they'll support us . . . a cake here, some surplus runner beans there. It all helps. It's all part of the continuing cycle of energy exchanges. Money is merely part of that cycle.

A $10,000 Master

But where does Reiki Healing fit into all this? In the US, the Reiki Alliance requires (or at least used to require) that its members pay a set amount to join. The fee to be paid before being accepted as a Master member was $10,000. It's necessary, they say, to maintain standards. As a Quality Assurance expert, I have to agree that 'you pays your money and you takes your choice', but since when has a high price tag guaranteed a high quality product or service? The cost of something is only part of the equation. And why should it always be measured is pounds or dollars? In classes I put it as follows:

* It is important that in giving Reiki treatments or classes we value our time and efforts. We have a living to make and deserve to be paid for the service we are providing. Note that it is not the Reiki that our customers are paying for . . . but our time, our expertise, our ability to listen and help others. Also note that payment can be 'in kind': a Reiki treatment in return for a massage or supply of fruit and veg.

* One thing we can receive 'in return' for Reiki is experience. Particularly as we are learning our craft. Apprenticeship is after all an established idea . . . and we wouldn't expect to pay a beginner as much as an established professional - be they blacksmith or healer.

* Part of the 'equation' is also commitment by the client or student. Why should we bust a gut if they are not doing their bit? Reiki is after all about encouraging everybody to take responsibility for their own life and health. A fair price tag for a treatment or training class is but one way of demonstrating this commitment. Sacrifices may have to be made - sometimes these need to be financial.

* One argument for the $10,000 Masters price tag is that even if we don't normally have such sums of money, if it's meant to be, it will come to us. I have no doubt that this can happen. I also respect those Reiki teachers who choose to charge such fees . . . and those who treat and train for donations . . . or for free. Such choices are part of our path. We will each learn what we need to from them.

So, Reiki *is* an exchange of energy. What we receive in return for each treatment or training session will depend on the needs of those involved in it. There are no rules - or where there are, things are rarely as simple as the standards makers would have us believe:

The problem with Rules

The financial aspect of Reiki is one of those areas where the worlds of spirituality and the conventional approach to life and business seem to clash head-on. I.e. it forces us, if we are honest with ourselves, to look at some of the ways we're brought up to do business. ARE all the rules and regulations (such as minimum costs) actually necessary or useful? More of this later (Chapter 33), but for now, a little bit about standards and Reiki.

My work with standards (I used to be chairman of a European standards committee and sat on other such groups) highlighted one or two particular problems with rules, with any instructions written down as 'the way to do something':

* There will always be situations which the rules haven't allowed for. E.g. how can someone with only one arm do the standard Reiki positions?

* They discourage the users from working out for themselves what's appropriate.

The best guidelines, rather than stating what you should and shouldn't do, describe the principles, give things to be aware of and help each reader to *understand* the issues involved. They state intent and suggest approaches . . . leaving the detailed 'how' up to you . . . so that you can take the here and now situation into account.

The above comments apply to rules in any walk of life, but are particularly relevant in Reiki where the whole objective is to help us each to become true to our selves . . . to do what *we* know to be right, here and now. How can any written set of rules, no matter how well written, or widely accepted, do this? *It depends what you put in them.* Perhaps we *could* have a Reiki 'Code of Practice' which encourages us to:

* Be aware of the expectation of each client and act accordingly. (In terms of time-keeping, use of treatment couch/bed, music, costs, etc)

* Allow the Reiki, through intuition, to guide you in hand positions, duration for each position, and other practical matters

i.e. maybe we cannot standardise on common sense and flexibility, but we CAN encourage it!

The spirit of any worthwhile law is it's divine law aspect. The heart of any rule is the mystic order beneath it. Thus the spirit of driving laws is that we love other road users unconditionally - we behave 'with due care and attention', we put 'the greater good' before our selfish desire to get from a to b in double quick time.

Likewise the spirit of Reiki is the flow of the energy itself. When our intent is to love unconditionally we enable this energy to flow within us - and whatever we focus our attention on. Any code of practice that encourages this process is going to help. Rules that attempt to restrict free flow of Reiki are, in contrast, likely to hold us back. What we charge or pay for our Reiki is but one issue to consider. Choose for yourself whether the letter of the law ($10,000) or the spirit of the law (cost to suit the moment) best fits your circumstances.

Reiki - Without Rules

18 - Self Treatments

One of the many beauties of Reiki is that you can treat yourself. Particularly useful for those who live alone, but helpful to everybody at some time. Part of the objective is, after all, to take responsibility for our own lives and health. A key feature of this is the actual act of giving ourselves the time and attention: to love ourselves. And don't we need it!

Many just beginning with Reiki self treatments report that they feel very little - at least compared to the sensations they experience in the Reiki I class. There are a number of factors at work here:

* Those at an early stage of their awareness path, even if they are keen to learn, may not be able to detect what is happening at a conscious level. This doesn't mean that the energy isn't 'going in' and doing what it needs to! Indications are that the Reiki will be helping to raise their awareness. After sufficient practice, the channel will be opened up and the level of conscious awareness will be sufficiently developed to enable these individuals to *feel* what the healing is doing. This may take months or many years. The more efforts have been made to 'face reality' and to accept and work with spiritual energies (in whatever form), the less actual (physical) practice of Reiki is likely to be needed before its effects can be felt.

* The group effect. In a class, the combination of many souls all connecting to The Universal energy at the same time tends to amplify the flow of energy and thus the effect for everybody in the group.

* The sharing effect. Even for a Reiki treatment or share between two people, the effects noticed are often significantly heightened compared to self treatment. This could be due to a resonance of energy - the sum being greater than the two parts. This might be because we find it easier to 'give' to others than to 'give' to ourselves.

With practise however, even self treatments can take us to a place of total peace and bliss.

Visualisation or Meditation?

It is not unreasonable to consider a Reiki self treatment as a meditation and/or visualisation. Certainly the three techniques can be merged very effectively. The following is just one possibility, the Appendix another. Explore any others that feel good for you.

Freeform

Sit or lie where you're physically safe. Put on some music that you find relaxing. Perhaps it includes the sounds of dolphins or creatures of the forest. Let your mind go with the creatures and/or sounds. Swim with the dolphins, fly with the birds. Whilst doing this, put your hands on your body in a comfortable position - if your heart's aching, place your hands there, if you have cold feet, hold them. If your mind wanders from the music let it follow your breathing or your heart-beat. Just focus your attention on the natural rhythm - at the point where you're holding your hands.

If thoughts come into your mind, let them. Let them come . . . and go. By not focusing on them, they'll disappear. Allow images to come into your mind too - colours, shapes . . . or general sensations. These you can focus on. Watch the colours and shapes move and change. Don't attempt to analyse or even describe them . . . just enjoy them. This is the Reiki energy moving around your mind, freeing up blockages, connecting the various bits together. Give your imagination full play - watch rainbows or angels, allow your awareness to float into other places or other realms. Wherever. Whenever. However. The idea is to experience freedom. A mind free from doubts, worries . . . from thoughts.

When the music stops, give yourself a few minutes to let the experience finish. Allow the colours to complete their 'show'. Open your eyes and take in what's around you . . . without losing the sense of peace and calm.

The above is an exercise, a practice in 'connecting' to the energy.

The more we are able to practice in this sort of way, the easier we will find it to reach that place of peace and calm. Whilst it can be used as a relaxation exercise, this is not its prime purpose. With Reiki it's not usually the intent to disconnect from the world around us in the way that the above exercise often does. Don't be too bothered about being disturbed. When we are connected through Reiki to our higher self, it takes more than a knock on the door to shatter our calm.

It probably depends on what you see as a meditation, but perhaps here we have a difference between this as a Reiki exercise and as a meditation. Whilst doing the Reiki we will be moving around (as we change hand positions) and it's OK to open our eyes from time to time and watch the fly on the lampshade. The eye shutting and inward focusing is only a means to an end - not an end it itself.

Walking, Dancing, Meditations

As we work to and through Reiki II, we find we can 'connect' without hands-on and the above practice can be taken off the bed or couch. By using the symbols to focus on the natural world for example, we can meditate with our eyes open. We are becoming more aware of the world around us. Connected to the energy of life within all things. One of the most powerful meditation experiences I had was one damp evening, looking out of my back door at my pond. A frog hopped out and sat a few feet away, motionless. I allowed my attention to be with the frog. I 'threw' by awareness as a ventriloquist might throw his voice. I sensed only what that frog was sensing. Fascinating. Powerful.

Likewise we talk of walking meditations, allowing ourselves to be *in* our steps and totally *with* wherever we're walking through. Not cut off from the world around but with heightened sight, sound, taste, touch and smell . . . of anything that is in the space surrounding us. With practice, this can be achieved not just in a country park, but also in a busy town centre!

Singing and dancing too can amount to a Reiki treatment and/or meditation - when we are fully *with* the music, in tune with it, in total harmony. A great way to help our thoughts rise above any other irrelevancies and to connect with the energy of the sound and music around us.

Reiki might well be used to *detach* us from things and thoughts which have got out of proportion in our minds and lives, but it does not *disconnect* us. On the contrary. The more we use Reiki, the more connected to everything around us we become. More aware of all . . . but without any emotional attachment. Some might say, we have the best of both worlds.

19 - Treating others

Is Reiki a therapy to be used alongside Reflexology, aromatherapy, etc? *Sometimes, but perhaps not in the same way.* It is important that we look at the intent of offering and receiving Reiki as a paid treatment. I offer Reiki treatments, but only as an introduction to Reiki, to give people a feel as to what to expect from Reiki healing. I might give a number of treatments to someone whilst they realise its power and potential. But the intent is to help them help themselves. As and when a given client is ready, often after one treatment, they'll take a First Degree Reiki course. I don't treat them to heal them. I give a treatment to demonstrate how they can treat themselves.

At the other extreme, there are those unable to take on their own healing. Even after a number of treatments some individuals will still be physically and/or mentally incapable of giving themselves self-treatments. But where is the line drawn? *There are no rules!* I would suggest that far more people *could* be shown how to treat themselves. The following comments are offered in support:

* Those who are physically unable to give themselves hands on treatments could be taught to 2nd degree level and shown how to send themselves 'absent' healing. Or, put another way, great benefit comes from visualisation exercises (such as those given in this book).

* Those with learning disabilities are often very intuitive. It is likely that many could easily take to giving hands-on treatments. Why not give them the attunements and let them spread their love more physically?

There are also reasons why treatments may be given rather than training:

* The patient wants to remain as such. Perhaps they've got a 'cushy number'. Why should they do the hard work if somebody else is

prepared to do it for them? If somebody doesn't want to get well, *that* is the issue that needs healing first.

* The patient *needs* to remain dependant. i.e. Their soul purpose is perhaps to learn humility, to learn to take. Such souls not only benefit from the physical healing but also benefit from an awareness of their situation.

* The therapist may not want them to take control of their own life. Hopefully this will not be the case, but the 'normal' view in society is still that a therapist (conventional or complementary) carries on treating a patient until they are 'better' . . . whatever that means! This approach is rarely in tune with the spirit of Reiki . . . except as in the above example.

Having said all that, there are many excellent Reiki Practitioners around, most doing a wonderful job. Many clients probably *do* need many treatments before they are willing and able to take control of their own healing. The healing role of the therapist is perhaps more of a teacher, educating the client into the ways of holistic lifestyle, helping them to see how they can improve their own health. This is what the best therapists (and doctors and nurses for that matter) have been doing all along.

Friends and Family

Much of the above discussion applies equally to friends and family. *Why* are we giving them healing treatments? Do they actually *need* it? Are we encouraging a dependency by 'giving' treatments all the time? . . . or is Reiki something that is shared between the family or group of friends, naturally, as and when required?

It is perhaps useful to see Reiki as part of an on-going relationship between people, rather than as a treatment that is given. It is not a commodity to be traded, but an energy to be exchanged.

None of these things really matter though. For as Reiki is given, so the energy itself will help raise the awareness of which of these issues (if any) is relevant. With Reiki, it all comes out in the wash.

Healing Hands

Many therapists in other disciplines, particularly massage and Reflexology recognise that the manipulations that they give to their clients are but part of their treatment. Similarly those receiving massage type treatments may well sense a significant difference between those therapist who are 'going through the motions' and those who are 'putting their heart and soul into it'. Any therapist, or nurse, who has their hands in contact with patient or client is already giving them a healing treatment too. The better a channel, the more powerful the healing aspect of the therapy. Such therapists thus take Reiki classes not to offer Reiki as a separate treatment, but to enhance what they know is a vital part of their service.

The following visualisation helps to develop the idea that a treatment is part of an on-going relationship - really getting to know someone. It's suitable for use when moving around a body giving a treatment:

The Facets of a Friend

Notice how that person looks so different when viewed from different angles. Look at the face from above, below and the side, see how different features become more prominent. Sense that with each change in physical appearance we are sensing a different aspect of that person. Each angle of view presents to us another facet of their character. Here the child, there the wise sage. From this perspective sadness or reflection, from another perspective a cheery disposition. We have all these, and many more, aspects to our personality. During a Reiki treatment, with the intimacy of physical and spiritual connection, is a great opportunity to explore the facets of a friend.

Other Positions

I was once told that I gave Reiki in my hugs. But of course! Reiki doesn't just flow through the hands, it flows between two people however they're physically connected.

It's great to experiment with Reiki. One very satisfying position is for the 'giver' to sit in a comfy chair with their legs apart and the 'receiver' to sit on the floor in-between the legs. The treatment then proceeds with hands onto the head and shoulders. What also happens is that Reiki flows from knees and thighs of the 'giver'. A great feeling. The 'receiver' can complete the circle and place their hands on the 'givers' feet so that both are giving and receiving.

With a partner, such shared experiences can become as intimate and intense as appropriate. The problem with many 'standard' Reiki treatment positions is that they are uncomfortable to hold for any length of time. So, instead adopt any position where both are comfortable and in contact - lying side by side embracing each other for example. Then just let the Reiki flow! What better way of showing your love for another human being? If you happen to be in bed at the time and fall asleep during the treatment, you may end up giving each other an all night, all over, Reiki!

Try this often powerful sharing position as an exercise:

Face to Face

Sit on the floor facing your partner and make eye contact. As Reiki helps us clear our minds of unnecessary clutter, so our eyes become clearer. Looking deep into the eyes of another is a way of connecting at a soul level. To enhance the feeling of 'communion' between you, place both hands together with your partner - palm to palm. Allow the energy to flow and to build up . . . and to take you wherever it needs to. Keep your eyes open and continue focusing your vision - inner and outer - on your partner. Allow your perception of this other being to change as you watch. Allow different features to seem more significant one moment only to fade into nothing the next. Perhaps you see a Buddhist monk before you - bless them, or a native American Indian - bow in greeting. See these beings as part of your partner, sharing key characteristics, wisdom, natural power. Lose yourself in the experience. As you are seeing so much in the face you're looking at, so they are seeing so much in yours. This is a deep sharing, reflecting a commitment to openness, a desire to find the truth in ourselves and each other.

The first time I did this, I found myself looking not just into the eyes of my healer friend but into the eyes of everyone I'd ever known! Even I described the experience, in my earlier days of Reiki, as 'weird'. Certainly it was a new experience to me and not one many have had. However, it happened and helped me to see things very differently.

Reiki and sex

From the above, it is clear that the level of connection between two people can be greatly enhanced by mutual Reiki treatments . . . particularly when we break the rules for positions and 'go with the flow'. I have often considered that true love is when we share with another intimately and intensely in mind, body and soul. Add Reiki to your lovemaking, and that's what you get! When two souls become one - as they do in Reiki, then we have the ideal setting for hearts and minds to become one too . . . it's all part of Unconditional Love, where there is no distinction between loving God, loving yourself and loving each other. In practice, fears will surface and preconceived ideas will have to be dealt with, but when both (or even just one of the couple) are able to let the Reiki flow, nothing cannot be handled . . . even the break-up of that relationship.

I was once asked, by a very attractive lady, oozing with sexual energy, "What about sex?" It was during a First Degree Reiki class, but the question was valid and had to be faced head on. I found myself answering that our sexuality is part of who and what we are. Sexual energy is one aspect of our spiritual energy. To deny our inherent manliness or femininity (or both) is to be untrue to our inner being. At the same time, society has imposed many conditions and unrealistic expectations when it comes to sex. So often we have dreams of a perfect partner and minds full of romantic slush. Such thoughts are rarely real.

The role of Reiki is thus to help us 'get real' with our view of partners, the opposite sex and of our sexuality. In Reiki we are able to rise above our conditioning and see things as they really are - to put our dreams into perspective. Even before I took up Reiki I had become a naturist to help me see human bodies as they're meant to be seen . . . as human bodies, not as some sex object. Beautiful as works of nature, whatever the size and shape of the individual. Reiki assists in this realisation process, helping us to love everybody *in an appropriate way.*

20 - Other uses

Having covered the use of Reiki for treatments to ourselves and other adults we now turn to its wider applications. It will come as no surprise to hear that 'there are no rules'. That isn't to say that Reiki is always appropriate. It might not be. Only by tuning into a given situation will we *know* what's needed there and then. So, use your Reiki to help with the tuning in process . . . but accept that actually giving treatments may not be relevant. We might, for example, be 'told' by our inner voice that it's not for us to get involved.

Children and Pregnant Women

Babies and young children are very receptive to Reiki. Since they have not been filled with conditioning, they have few mental blocks to get in the way of natural energy flow. Reiki is not so much to restore them to balance but to restore you (in giving the treatment) and their environment to a calm, peaceful, one in which the child is more naturally 'at home'.

It is worth, at this point, looking again at the issue of intent. We may *want* a child to stop crying . . . but is that for the greater good? Babies cry for a reason. Before we try to impose our will on this new human being we can use Reiki to help us tune into this reason . . . and act accordingly. Maybe we are over-reacting? Maybe we are being too hard on ourselves. Using Reiki (by giving ourselves and/or the baby a treatment) will help us see the truth of a given situation . . . which may, or may not, enable the baby to stop crying!

Having had the pleasure of teaching a pregnant women (or two) I can attest to the wonder of being in the presence of a new being. There is no doubt in my mind that the attunements involved not just myself and my student but also her unborn child . . . perhaps the wisest of the three of us. There is also little doubt that this youngest of people was teaching us as much, if not more, than I was teaching others . . . about purity, about unconditional love.

Perhaps the principle of respect is relevant here. Beings of any age are worthy of our utmost respect . . . unborn babies are no exception. Before treating, or attuning, a pregnant women, it is wise to ask the consent of the child . . . by tuning into its presence and sensing its needs.

Not Just People!

The same is true of animals and plants. By 'tuning in' I mean allowing ourselves to sense the life within the other being. To focus our attention on it. With our hands around it we will be in Reiki Healing mode and thus able to make a connection. Our inner voice will speak for it.

We can thus assist newly repotted plants, germinating seeds and poorly pets. As when treating humans, we may sense the flow of energy as a warming in our hands. We might also get a sense of hurt or know that we need to provide water. The language of Reiki is universal; beyond words.

On inanimate objects too, Reiki may prove useful; particularly electronic and mechanical things. As an electronics engineer I know how sensitive modern electronics are. It is no surprise to me that photocopiers always break down when you need them most urgently. If, by contrast, we approach them radiating calm and peace, they're far more likely to work as required. My students have reported, amongst other things, a fax machine that started working after a Reiki treatment and a car that went many miles up the M6 without a petrol tank! Such things only happen when they need to, but with Reiki the unexpected often occurs.

Reiki is also useful for food. Giving our food and drink a quick treatment before we eat might be considered as the New Age equivalent to a blessing - both being an opportunity to show our gratitude for our sustenance. At another level, Reiki can help us face the 'dos' and don'ts' of nutritional advice. For example:

Do Reiki Masters eat Meat?

Some do, some don't. There are no rules - and many real issues around the question of vegetarianism. Whilst still a meat eater I have to admit to eating far less now than I used to 'pre-Reiki', but not for any particular ethical reason . . . it just happened. After regularly enjoying a liver casserole most weeks I just found it wasn't right, for me one particular week, to buy any more liver. Next to go, at least on a regular basis, was ham. Because it was no longer right for me or my body . . . and to justify it more than that is to let the logical mind take over.

To eat according to a set of rules is to over-simplify the reality. There are many other issues involved. For example:

* Leather free footwear? What's the alternative? Man-made? From what? Using what limited resources, producing what by-products? Assuming (OK some say we shouldn't) we keep cows for milk, it is plain daft not to use their hides when they die!

* Water use. To keep cows where there is little water is again plain daft. Yes, the inefficiency of watering plants to feed herds of cattle is unsustainable. But what about natural pastures? The Welsh hills, the moor lands of Yorkshire and Devon - plenty of grasses (of one sort or another) requiring little extra water or food to bring up healthy sheep. Such animals *are* efficient use of land and resources . . . these area of our countryside probably couldn't support any vegetable crops.

* I was surprised to see that the Vegetarian Society supports Genetic Engineering in principle, arguing that it offers improvement in the nutritional value of vegetarian food and the ease with which it can be produced. Yes, it warns that safeguards are needed but . . .

Surely the main issue is one of intent - what makes the GE companies do it? Are they really driven by 'the greater good' or their desire for profits?

There are SO many issues here. There can be no answer coming from any single campaign or belief. The holistic approach to life needs to embrace ALL factors. Well done to the Vegetarian Soc. for raising awareness of some of the issues, but we need to bring in sustainability and awareness of damage to plant-life etc.

The real question to be asked, with vegetarianism as with any other issue is "*are we working WITH nature, or against it?*". Are we going with the flow of the universe or trying to impose our will on other beings? Note that such questions do not rule out Genetic Engineering - but only when we're guided to do it in truth.

Which means what? The trouble is, the gurus at Monsanto will say that they ARE doing it for the greater good . . . and they ARE, in truth, doing *their* best. There are no rules. Those who DO sense dangers may well have a duty to challenge the integrity of those who would act as God . . . without being in communion with God. It's a complex question, one probably beyond a mortal mind to answer. So we need a way of helping us to eat healthily:

You are What You Eat

Next time you're eating, try this visualisation (taken from my book 'Rosy Tinted Glasses'):

Take a bite or a mouthful of whatever you have in front of you. As you put it to your mouth breath in any aroma it has: perhaps it's a mature cheese or a spicy curry. Or maybe you've been handling fresh apples and that unique smell of their waxy surface is all over your hands. Breath it in. Savour it as you would the bouquet of a good wine.

Once in your mouth, roll the tongue around sensing the texture. Perhaps it's the crispness of the apple or a cheese that dissolves in your mouth. Taste and feel the food as a flavour, as something that has given itself for you. As it dissolves, as you swallow, imagine it becoming part of you. No longer a separate plant or whatever, but goodness, energy.

Sense the energy. What sort of energy is it? Be with the food as it was whilst being grown. Perhaps it was a lamb on the natural pasture of a Welsh hill bouncing with pure vitality. Or ears of wheat or oats swaying gently in the breeze of a balmy British summer evening . . . or the intense heat of Florida or Spain ripening your orange or clementine. BE with it. Take yourself to the source of your meal, allow it's energy to permeate your being as it's physical energy releases itself into your body.

Now allow your mind to sense any other energies of your meal. Perhaps it's a cake that's been lovingly prepared by your mum, or bread baked individually by traditional methods. Take in these other energies. Have they added to the original nourishment of the ingredients . . . or not? Perhaps you know who made the dish you're eating . . . and they know you . . . and enjoyed the creative process. All this positive energy is in the food as we eat it. Savour it, appreciate it . . . it is becoming part of you!

Of course, this is the case whatever you're eating. ALL the energies that went into your food will now become part of you . . . we absorb it all . . . positive or negative. Doing this exercise regularly will help us to think of food as vibrational energy, rather than as chemicals. It will help us to tune into each thing we eat and assess whether it really is good for us or not. Not whether it nominally has or has not got some particular nutrient or vitamin, but whether it's a natural, nourishing ENERGY or not. If the food has been force grown, produced under slave labour, travelled half way around the world, processed by those who don't care and sold for the highest price, what sort of energy will it have then? The best way to choose your food is to meditate on these ideas and let your intuition, enhanced by Reiki, guide you to what best meets your energy needs . . . it's far more reliable than any list of 'good for you's.

21 - Other energies?

Some Reiki Master offer attunements in other Energies - Seichem and Karuna (TM)* being two of the more well known. They say that these attunements enable us to access other aspects of the Universal Energy. Maybe it's a matter of definition and perhaps I'm being pedantic, but if Reiki is *The Universal* Energy, does it not embrace *all* aspects of the energy of life? Reiki is already "much more than everything, much less than nothing" . . or at least it is in my experience and by my definition!

* Karuna Reiki is trademarked by the International Centre for Reiki Training.

There are a number of issues here which are worth reflecting on:

Broadening the Channel

It certainly seems to be true that the more Reiki we use and channel, be it in treatments or attunements, then the broader the spread of aspects of the energy we become able to channel. Each mystic order experience and/or blessing opens us up that bit more . . . in whatever way we most need opening up at that time. It *may* be that how we're attuned (by what procedure, under what name, etc.) does result in some *specific* channel being opened up in us, but I doubt it will be the same channel in each person so attuned . . . if only because everybody is different.

Divide and Conquer?

By way of an introduction to Chapter 26 - New Science:

Until very recently it has been a human need to categorise and label, to break things down into their constituent parts. The reductionist approach. The theory was that only by dividing things into bits could we understand them. Increasingly all branches of science (and a few others!) are recognising that life is a system . . . the whole greater than its constituent parts. By breaking things down we miss the essential One-ness of life . . . at any level. There is a danger, in defining different aspects of the Universal Energy, that we do the same with Reiki.

Besides, why do we need to isolate and separate the 'energy for peace' from the 'earth energy' or 'water energy'? Some seem to want to, presumably because it helps them to feel in control of it all. And to be fair, maybe it is important to recognise the difference aspects of The Universal Energy, so that we can better understand what it is and it's potential. But do we need to label it? And can we, even if we want to, really isolate one bit from another? My experience is that the Universe is in control. It decides which aspect is needed. I doubt it cares what we call it.

There are other courses too that attune us in light energy or other realms of healing - 'Purple Flame', for example. Many of these do indeed offer us a connection to The Universe, to our inner/higher self. Some people may feel the need to try some or all these different forms. All paths lead to the same One-ness, so let's not get hung-up on what we call it. Reiki has been enough for me . . . but it might not be for you.

REIKI II:

THE NEXT DIMENSION

22 - Second Degree:

an introduction

What Reiki I does at the physical level, Reiki II does at the mental level. i.e. it's a way of focusing healing energy not into a body part but into our thought processes. Although often presented as 'Absent Healing' this use is but one facet of Second Degree Reiki.

To understand Reiki II intellectually we need to be comfortable with the idea that every thought and feeling that ever was, is and might be exists in some form of universal consciousness: i.e. the eternal now contains all past and all future. We also need to be comfortable with Reiki Energy being the energy that transcends every other form of energy: atomic bonds, gravity, time, etc. Thus, by channelling Reiki we are connecting our conscious mind into this collective consciousness. We are opening ourselves to every thought and feeling from all times and spaces . . . or at least, those we need to access.

We can now begin to see what is possible with Reiki II: access to other times and other places. Besides 'healing at a distance' we can also connect to events of our past . . . to help us come to terms with them, and connect to a possible future to help us prepare for it. Note that we are not actually changing the past or future, the Reiki Healing is happening in our minds, changing our thought processes to bring them into line with what really happened and what's likely to happen.

Likewise, we are not actually 'healing at a distance'. We are merely focusing Reiki at another location, that whatever needs to happen is encouraged to do so. At the level that Reiki works, there is no 'here' or 'there'. All places are One.

So, how does it work and what can it do?

23 - Symbols as tools

Reiki Healing has, associated with it, some symbols. Depending on who teaches you, it may be 3 symbols at Second Degree and one extra at Masters or somewhat more than that. Despite considerable research and many, often conflicting, opinions the origins of these symbols is uncertain. Similar symbols can be found in Indian, Chinese, Tibetan and of course Japanese cultures. As Usui rediscovered the healing art that became Reiki, he may well have been 'shown' symbols that have influenced a number of cultures and religions. Perhaps this common ancestry is more important than knowing precisely which symbols Usui himself used.

As Usui's symbols were taught and learnt through time and 'handed down' successive generations, so variants arose. It has reached the stage now where one symbol learnt on one branch of one lineage may not even be recognisable by a student on a different branch of Usui's family tree. Although many branches insist that their way of drawing the symbol is the correct one, the fact is that most, probably all, these variants work. As far as which symbols are the right symbols we have to conclude that *there are no rules.*

So what *is* a Reiki symbol, what does it do and how does it work? *Nobody really knows!* Or at least I've yet to hear a fully satisfactory explanation. They can however be considers as tools, as keys to helping us connect to the Reiki energy as and when we need to.

Are the Reiki Symbols sacred or secret? *For many years the symbols used in Reiki were considered both sacred and secret.* It was thought that they should be seen and used only by those formally initiated into their use - e.g. through Reiki II training. Even now Reiki attunements are usually seen as sacred acts. The whole point of the symbols is that they help us to connect to our higher self - a very sacred, divine, event.

Thus the Reiki Symbols are not mere gimmicks to play with without some appreciation as to their power - which can often be immense. But neither are they now secret. In recent years they have been published (e.g. in Diane Sterns' "Essential Reiki") with the intent of improving access to Reiki. Having the symbols in print encourages active debate amongst Reiki practitioners. It enable those who *have* been taught the symbols to compare their versions and to share experiences. I've found that such sharing provides invaluable learning opportunities. By sharing 'our' symbols with those that other Reiki folks have been given, we begin to see just how different they can be in detail, yet how they all achieve the same end.

Why should this be? *Because a true symbol transcends culture, history and other human divisions.* A true symbol is universal. It is a pattern that exists at all dimensional levels. i.e. it is something that is predominantly the same whether seen at the microscopic level (atomic), the human scale or at the macroscopic level (e.g. cosmic). It has the same meaning whether used in an Eastern culture, a Western society, in the 21st century or in ancient Egypt. This meaning is beyond words, it cannot be defined. It just *is.*

Thus, true symbolism means that when we invoke that symbol we connect to all dimensions. A true symbol *is* a link between our dimension, our time, our culture and all other times, dimensions and cultures. A description of symbolism describes, as perfectly as any words can, what Reiki symbols do.

This then begs the question as to whether the Reiki Symbols are true symbols. This, to me, is debatable; at least with respect to 3 of the 4 symbols I was taught. It is, in my experience, true of a 5th symbol, the Raku or lightning bolt, but some lineages (such as mine) don't (or at least didn't) consider it part of the Usui teaching!

And yet the symbols work. When we use them there is little doubt that we are able to connect more easily, more powerfully with the universal energy. Why should this be? It would seem that these particular patterns have an inherent power to them. Or do they? Two other experiences may help to explain what's happening:

Focusing Our Attention

By using a symbol, any symbol, we are focusing our mind. We are encouraging our thought processes to stop their ramblings and to allow the mind to become a channel for love. Maybe this is their main function - to give our minds something to occupy it, so that the energy can flow freely between different levels of consciousness. Whilst true symbols may have an extra effect, any personal symbol, or indeed visualisation, can achieve this. It could be argued that visualising, say a golden orb during meditation or a physical Reiki treatment, amounts to using a symbol. Given the very real Mystic Order experiences that often result from such practices, we have to conclude that there is some truth in such a theory.

A Tool to Learning

Those who have been practising or teaching Reiki for some time and/or with some intensity may find that they no longer need the symbols. Connecting with our higher self is automatic. We can, at will, become at one with our higher selves and allow Reiki to flow in and through us in any situation. We thus have to conclude that the symbols are not actually necessary to make the connection. They can however be very useful during our early days of accessing our inner, energetic selves. Because they give our mind something to focus on they amplify our intent during such practice - to become one, to rise above a purely physical form and embrace our true selves.

We are usually taught however that each Reiki symbol has a particular purpose, that it connects us to a specific aspect of the energy. *If that theory is useful to you, use it.* It is not my experience. As is discussed in Chapter 21 - Other Energies, I question the usefulness of labelling and categorising different aspects of the Universal Energy. *Keep it Simple.* My experience is that we connect and access whichever bit of the energy we need at any one time. OK, one symbol may resonate with one aspect of the energy more than another and could thus be more useful in some situations - e.g. the Sei He Ki (the 2nd symbol) for emotional situations. But when it boils down to it, all the so called different meaning and uses to each symbol are really different ways of saying the same thing. Whether we say 'Harmony in mind, body and soul' or 'connecting heaven to earth' or 'turning on the power' we have the same general intent . . . to become one with our higher self, to connect to our spiritual essence, to have God live in us. Rather than get bogged down in semantics, let's just do it and enjoy it! Use whatever symbol feels right for you . . . if any.

Spirals

The Reiki Symbol that most readily demonstrates true symbology is the First Symbol, Cho Ku Rei. Inevitably when teaching it in Second Degree classes, students will point out that it reminds them of snail's shells, or whirlpools, or the Milky Way or some other natural, or indeed man-made object or phenomena. On inspection we see that the part of the Cho Ku Rei that matters is the spiral - a truly universal pattern, the back cover of this book being but one example of many:

* In art from around the world (e.g. Maori engravings) and across the centuries (cave paintings) we see spirals in one form or another. Always drawing us into the picture, helping us to connect with other times and places.

* In the natural world spirals occur in many places - leaves positioned around a stalk, stars in a galaxy, etc.

* Many who experience a NDE, a Near Death Experience, will report travelling through a tunnel, a corridor, spiralling towards another world.

* In the bodies of all living matter we have DNA - the famous double helix that holds our genes - the very blue-print of who and what we are. Inter-twining spirals. In bananas, in gorillas, in us. Spirals are common to all life forms. They connect us.

Few of these spirals are flat. Most have a depth to them . . . even if they're drawn on a flat surface! They nearly always seem alive, often revolving, drawing us in. So it is with the Cho Ku Rei. We are taught to use it by making it part of us, by *being* it. It is three dimensional . . . at least. One of the most powerful visualisations I do is as follows:

Spirals

Draw (in your mind) a spiral around yourself, wrapped around your whole body. Imagine it reaching up into the heavens and down into the heart of the earth. Feel in revolving in one direction, drawing you up, then in the other direction, taking you down. Then revolving in both directions at once, connecting you to the physical realm of our planet and to the spiritual realm of energy. Now visualise the spiral expanding, getting bigger and bigger until it has become the Milky Way. Let it get smaller again, taking in all other spiral forms around us. Then let it get smaller still, as a coil up and down our spine. Then smaller still becoming a strand of DNA in our body, becoming each and every strand of DNA is us . . . and in all living things. Feel the spiral expand and contract yet still remaining this universal symbol. Without beginning, without end. Reminding us that we are one with creation itself.

This is the power of a real symbol.

24 - Absent Healing

When did you last send somebody love in a letter or over the phone? Or wish somebody luck or send them sympathy? All of these are examples of absent healing. We're doing it all the time. Reiki II merely provides us with a tool for connecting more powerfully with others. In fact there is nothing new or different in Reiki . . . there doesn't need to be. We already have the inherent ability to heal ourselves and to send love. It's just that we tend to overlook these abilities, perhaps even to deny them. The value of Reiki II training is thus to help us to appreciate these skills, to practice and develop them.

Distant healing, like hands-on, is a sharing, not a 'give' and 'take'. Quite often, in 'sending a Reiki', we will find that we've had a significant treatment ourselves. Perhaps we've connected to the recipient in a way we've never experienced before, or sensed something about them . . . or ourselves . . . that comes as a shock. Sending Reiki isn't like sending a package of potions, it is making a connection with another person at a soul level, beyond thoughts and facts, but embracing them. 2nd Degree training normally gives you a taste of this, allowing us to feel the, often profound, sense of being joined to another person, who is not physically present.

How to Do It

A typical distance healing consists of the following:

* Setting our intent - i.e. clearing our mind of any pre-conceived idea as to the outcome of the treatment, and of any other thoughts. If clearing our mind is difficult, then an affirmation can be used, e.g. "I intend to channel love and light to X, for the greater good". As with hands-on healing (see Chapter 13), it is worth remembering that we're not doing this to impose our will on a situation! Nor to bring about a 'cure'. The universe knows what's needed, we're just helping that process along.

* Tuning In - getting a sense of connection to the person we'd like to send healing to. If we're not able to picture that person in our mind's eye, then look at a photo of them or hold something belonging to them. Anything that identifies the 'recipient'.

* Checking it's OK - At this point we'll probably have a sense as to whether giving this treatment is appropriate. If we can't seem to connect to that person, then they could be 'engaged' in other important work. Or it might be that we're being 'told' not to proceed - at least at this time. Ask the question "Is it right for me to treating X here and now?" and listen to your inner voice for an answer. Don't push it. Remember that we're doing this for the greater good. If however we can feel the Reiki flowing in us and that we are 'with' our 'client' then we can proceed. Obviously the chance of this being the case will be greatly enhanced if we've previously agreed a suitable time for the treatment between us.

* 'Sending'. For a physical treatment it's useful to have a cuddly toy to use as a proxy. Hold that toy in the position you'd like to send the healing to - eyes, stomach, legs, etc. The full set of positions (as given in Chapter 10) can be used, but usually for less time than we'd maintain for a physical treatment. It's also more usual in absent healings to focus treatments to particular places - allowing our intuition to guide us to those spots. These differences tend to lead to a shorter, more focused, treatment - because we're not also satisfying needs of touch and companionship.

Thinking Globally?

As I was first drafting this section, the situation in the former Yugoslavia was causing concern to many. Whilst completing the final edit, Iraq and Israel were troubled areas. Always, it seems, there are places in need of help. These days this is provided by peace campaigners and 'light workers' enabling and encouraging us to all pray for peace in such trouble spots around the world.

There is little doubt that many are suffering in such conflicts. There is also increasing evidence that when enough people focus their loving attention on a global crisis it can help in its resolution. But the situation may not be quite as it is presented to us. After a few years of Reiki (or equivalent practice), we begin the see the spiritual perspective to global issues and to the large scale disasters we now have fed to us daily by the media.

Awareness is key. One thing that's happening here is that we are all becoming more aware of all that *is* happening around the globe. This is part of the process many of us need to go through - acceptance of the extremes of human behaviour and natural events.

There is a major paradox here. Whether the 'disaster' is human or man-made (e.g. earthquake or war) we might have two opposing views on it:

* Detachment. Unless we are physically involved in the affected part of the world, what good does it do for us to feel responsible? Getting all worked up by it, however atrocious the images we're being fed, helps no one, least of all us. We are responsible for how we think and feel. Any judgement and anger is merely feeding the human crisis. If we want to bring about peace on earth, the best place to start is within. Charity begins at home. Peace begins in our own minds.

* We are one. There is no separation between 'us' and 'them' . . . whether 'they' are the victims of floods or ethnic cleansing . . . or those who perpetrate such crimes against humanity. We cannot deny these events or the human beliefs that lie behind them. To this extent we *are* responsible for the wars and atrocities in the world today. The bigotry and closed minds we see responsible for so much pain and suffering is a reflection of our own closed minds - yours and mine. Blaming others achieves nothing. In judging others we judge ourselves.

So, on one hand we are not responsible for human disasters, on another we are! A typical paradox of life. *Both* sides of the story are true. Before Reiki I would have allowed myself to get caught up in the political background to a world crisis, or fumed at the injustice of it all. Neither reaction helps. But often such reactions are necessary - as we work through our own issues that such world crises trigger within us.

Reiki - Without Rules

Everything that happens around us, in society, is a reflection of what's going on within us. We are interconnected. It is widely accepted psychologically that those who think like victims often become victims. This would tend to support the idea that we choose our life on this planet. If we need to experience pain and suffering we choose to be victims. If we need to experience perceived superiority, maybe we'll become soldiers in a totalitarian regime.

We could take this idea a step further and apply it to natural disasters too. We each, at some level, *choose* to be present at the time and place of a tornado or volcanic eruption. Perhaps we *need* such an experience to help us find our inner strength and to be more appreciative of the true necessities of life - water, shelter, friends we can trust. There is a reason, a soul purpose, behind everything that happens to us. Personally. Yes, global issues are being resolved too, but as individuals, the battles and devastation that matter most are the inner conflicts - the struggle within our minds as we try to find our inner strength and wisdom.

So, how can we use Reiki to help us respond to the 'horrendous' scenes we see on the TV?

* Turn off the news and do a Reiki treatment instead. We feed ourselves far too many images of horror and destruction, which is totally out of proportion to the extent of disasters in the world. Yes, we need to be aware of what's happening, but we also need to balance the 'negative' news with the positive - subscribe to 'Positive News' and read of all the 'good' things that are happening in the world. (See Contacts section).

* "Just for today I will not judge". Whenever we start labelling something as 'good', 'bad', 'horrendous', atrocious', etc. remember that these are merely labels, signs of our own judgmental way of thinking. Use Reiki to help rise above these reactions and to see the bigger picture. One man's meat is another man's poison.

* Allow the Reiki to help us identify and work through our own issues that are triggered by world crises. Perhaps stories of abuse trigger thoughts from our own past which we need to face up to? Perhaps

we have some pent up resentment of authority figures which we need to release? By giving ourselves Reiki with such intents in mind, we can (albeit slowly) bring peace to our own mind. In doing so, we *are* doing our bit to bring about peace on earth.

* Recognise that chaos is a natural thing: Part of the process of breaking apart the old so that something new (and better) can be created. This applies to the natural world, to governments, to relationships . . . and to the way our own mind works. Chaos Theory is a major area for development in most areas of science and even in economics. Try the 'Scrabbled Egg' exercise in Chapter 31.

* Perhaps we *do* feel drawn to do something in response to a given catastrophe. Other than make a donation, or take ourselves off there and get involved 'on the ground' how can we help?

Whilst it is probably not our place to determine how a given conflict (or natural disaster) should be resolved, we can 'shed some light' on that situation and pray that God's Will Be Done. Try the following exercise as a variant of your absent healing practice:

Spreading Love & Light

Close your eyes and breathe deeply. Think and feel 'peace, love and light' - in whatever way you find brings about the deepest sense of calm and one-ness. Perhaps a pure white light spreading from your heart or crown. Feel the power and truth of Universal Peace spread throughout your mind and body. Allow the light to evaporate any irrelevant thoughts.

Now allow your mind to tune into the given global situation - be it war, famine, forest fire, or whatever triggers your concern. Allow an image to form and develop in your mind - the sights, sounds, smells, tastes and other sensations. Be with them, allow any emotions to surface - have a good sob if necessary. Whatever you need. Allow the 'picture' to develop or change - perhaps it becomes a picture of your own past. Be with it, tune into the new time and place and again allow out whatever feelings surface. THIS is the 'disaster' for you.

Whatever the situation that's now in your minds eye, focus the pure white light of love and peace at it. Feel the people involved enveloped by a deep and utter sense of harmony, of respect, of acceptance for each other and the world around them. Stay with the image. Whenever any darkness comes into view focus the light at it and 'see' it turn grey, then white, then become part of the overall Oneness. If a particular colour feels more appropriate, allow IT to flow through the picture, bringing with it a sense of serenity or calm. The divine presence IS in all things, in all situations. Through such focused meditations we enable that love and light to break through the doubts and denials, fears and anger, of all those involved. It is not our place to exert our personal wills on others, but divine love is ever present, divine wisdom knows how to move forward . . . and will guide all those now prepared to listen.

This exercise might last just a few seconds whilst watching a news programme or could be the basis of a group meditation over a much longer period. Be wary of taking in too much from the reported news story - turn off those images and allow the higher self to show you what's *really* happening.

Not only will such an exercise prevent some of the previous feeling of helplessness, but it also helps our own progress towards inner peace and thus makes a real difference to mankind's future on earth.

25 - Psychic Powers

You may have gathered by now that as we practice Reiki so we develop our psychic powers. Just as Healing is an inherent ability which we are now re-learning to use, so too are other psychic abilities. Some of us seem to be drawn to develop some skills more than others, but you can be sure that Reiki will bring our abilities to our attention and encourage us to develop and apply them . . . often in no uncertain terms! There are too many different skills to go into in this book, but to give you a flavour:

Dowsing

In 1987 I was a scientist and engineer through and through. Everything could be explained. Life was logical. And then I found I could dowse. I experienced the sensation of identifying a recently broken bone in somebody I'd never met before . . . by holding a pendulum over their body. My mind couldn't explain it, but it had happened. My exploration into the world outside of conventional science had begun. And I haven't looked back since . . . well, only to make sure I've learn my lessons from the past.

Dowsers sense energies in other things . . . including people. A skilled dowser can tell you what pipes, wires, or natural flows of water are under your land. They can even do it from maps. My dowsing high-light was to detect the bug in a computer program by dowsing over a listing of the program!

Since taking up Reiki I find I don't need a rod or pendulum, I just *know* what I need to know. A dowser is sensitive to particular vibrations and uses his twigs (or whatever) to amplify the signal so that it's visible. By asking questions in his mind he can 'tune in' to more specific energy types. It is a natural ability which many have, but some have in abundance. Maybe we all have this ability . . . and could save digging a lot of unnecessary holes if we were to use it more.

Telepathy

How often have you known who was on the phone before you picked it us? How often have you found yourself thinking of somebody you hadn't seen in years only to have a letter or call from them the next day? We are all telepathic. We already 'pick up' the thoughts of others. At present it might only be people we've a strong connection with. At present we might only know that they're thinking of us, without being knowing any more than that. But it's there. The connection is real and transcends space. If we are 'close' to someone, we are *always* close to them, no matter how far away they are physically. A true 'connection' is at the soul level and beyond limitation.

It is this connection which is enhanced through Reiki practice. It is this ability to 'pick up' what other people are thinking and feeling that is improved through 'absent healing' practice. As we develop this ability we find we can connect more readily to more people. We no longer need to have an especially strong connection with them beforehand . . . and we can begin to sense some detail in the 'messages' we receive.

So we are mind-readers? *Yes!* Does that bother you? Why? If we are honest and open with ourselves and others, what have we to fear from having our minds read? If we live in truth, say what we mean and mean what we say, what are mind readers going to find out that we're not willing and able to tell them face to face? Those who don't like the idea of widespread telepathy have something to hide.

To some, including me, the idea of telepathy being a way of life is appealing. When we know what others are thinking and feeling there will be do place for lies or deceit. A world where we are all honest and open will be free of all hurt that goes with these human conditions. And think of all the time and energy that will be saved when we don't have to read between lines all the time and interpret hidden agendas. Becoming telepathic is part of becoming one. By recognising that we are all interconnected, we realise that's there no point trying to pull the wool over the eyes of others . . . for in doing so we only deceive ourselves.

The following may help others appreciate and develop their telepathic abilities:

* To 'tune into' somebody we often only need to think about them, but looking at their picture and/or holding an object of theirs will help. If we only have a name, then just hold that in mind. The universe will do the rest.

* Telepathy is a 'transmission' of energy. Thoughts and feelings with a powerful emotional content are thus the ones that we receive most readily - like when we know a loved one has had an accident. Information with no meaning is unlikely to be transferred. i.e. the message needs to be one we *need* to know. We might, for example, sense that we don't have to rush to get to an airport or station to pick somebody up at a pre-arranged time. We'll allow life to take it's course and get there when we can . . . to find that their plane or train was delayed . . . and we arrive together. Sub-consciously we knew what we needed to know . . . and acted accordingly. The less cluttered our conscious minds with "should do . . . " and "this is because" type thoughts the easier we'll go with the flow and pick up the messages we need.

If (when?) we get good enough at it, we'll even be able to save on phone bills!

Clairvoyance & Clairaudience

Perhaps you're already able to detect the presence of a departed soul? Perhaps, when you allow yourself, you can hear or see relatives or friends who have died . . . or other spirit forms. Again, it is an ability we all have to some degree.

Whilst it is debatable exactly *what* we're seeing and hearing, that's probably a matter of definition and belief . . . which is not appropriate here. The point is, we are picking up a thought, feeling or more physical manifestation from someone who is no longer alive - in the same way as we sense a telepathic message. Given that Reiki connects us to all time and all space this is perhaps not particularly surprising. These things happen for a reason. Maybe it happens once or twice to 'prove' to us that the souls of our loved ones do live on. Or maybe we've been given this gift to enable us to help others make peace with family and friends who were 'taken from them'. Reiki is likely to enhance such abilities or to help us acknowledge them.

It's worth pointing out here that those in this line of work (Clairvoyants, Mediums, etc) refer to the passing of messages from the spirit world as 'channelling'. They become channels for information, energy, from that world to this . . . in exactly the same way as anybody practising Reiki provides a channels from the energy level to this physical human level. There is however a difference which may be significant: as clairvoyants (or clairaudients) we are channels for a particular departed human being. We are channels of the energy associated with that person. For exchange of personal feelings, for allowing their loved ones to let them go, this is fine. However, be aware that any information obtained in this way is only as 'good' as it might have been from that person when they were alive. If we make a connection with the spirit of a particular individual and restrict ourselves only to 'hearing' or 'seeing' what that being has to tell us, we may not be getting the full picture. Our eccentric great aunt doesn't suddenly come the wisest being around just because she's died!

For this reason, I personally don't have any 'Spirit Guides' as such. many healers do . . . and no doubt find extremely helpful. To connect to the wisdom of a genuine native American Indian, for example, could indeed provide inspiration beyond measure. And maybe that guide isn't so much providing information themselves as channelling guidance from other parts of the collective consciousness? It may be that the idea of Spirit Guides is a useful way of explaining the profundity of messages they we are getting - our minds being more able to accept that some ancient sage might know all this . . . . but that we don't, as if somehow they are more worthy than us.

Again, it probably boils down to beliefs and definitions which, like rules, can be far more trouble than their worth. I'd just ask the question - if we can get the truth direct from source (i.e. communicate directly with the universe), then why bother with an intermediary?

Positive Thinking

It could be argued that affirmations and positive thinking are examples of psychic power: mind over matter. Creating what we think. We can certainly use affirmations and visualisations to help turn what could be negative thoughts into worthwhile positive progress on our spiritual journey. For example our nagging mind trying to make itself heard. We've all heard it: "But, you *shouldn't* do that". "But what about . . . ", "But . . . " On and on it goes disturbing our intended peace. Old habits die hard. For that's all it is. Our conscious mind not wanting to let go of the thoughts it developed and has clung to for so long. So, we have to make it easier. The following visualisation may be helpful:

Turn Buts to Butterflies

You're intent on calming your mind, but even with plenty of self Reiki you find the old "Buts" butting into your thoughts:

Imagine the "but" as a thought, feel its presence in your mind. Allow this thought to develop wings. Big, beautiful coloured wings. It flits and flutters away. Every time an unwanted thought surfaces, picture it turning from its bug like chrysalis state into a butterfly of rare and exotic qualities. Each one circling a garden of wonderful plants with pretty blooms and heavenly scent. It disappears into the distance leaving our mind full of the sights, smells and sounds of nature's peace.

If even this visualisation isn't enough, include this affirmation "Turn Buts to Butterflies". Keep saying it until the old habits stop butting in.

26 - New Science

Reiki Energy can be 'explained' in both religious and scientific terms. Besides being God, it is also the 'The Collective Consciousness' (of psychologists, especially Jung) and the 'Grand Unifying Theory' that science now believes links all other known energies - atomic attraction, gravity, etc. Certainly few who work daily with sub-atomic physics or with the maths of the cosmos will deny the possibility of parallel worlds or other dimensions to time-space. The 3D world in which most humans live is but a very small bit of the Universe. We constrain ourselves to it only by our limited and limiting beliefs.

Even a fair review of the many developments in a whole spread of scientific fields is beyond the scope of this book. Anyone with an enquiring, scientific, mind who still needs theories is invited to read some of the following authors:

- Fritjof Capra - from a perspective of physics. Originally best known for "The Tao of Physics", but with many books since. "The Web of Life" has also been widely acclaimed.

- Rupert Sheldrake - with a biological perspective

- Deepak Chopra - with a healing perspective

- Murry Hope - with a metaphysical perspective

- James Gleick - with a mathematical perspective

- Richard Bach - inspired fiction containing much higher truth

- Ken Wilbur - philosophy brought into a spiritual perspective

A few, to me key, books by these and other relevant authors are listed in the *Reference* section.

Thus many features of more recent scientific thinking can do much to help our logical mind accept Reiki and its effects. For example:

Reiki - Without Rules

As Above, So Below

The concept of fractals is fairly simple: any object can be described by a single equation which applies at all levels - from microscopic to macroscopic. Take the humble fern as an example: if we see a picture of one splay of fern, without any scale, it is very difficult to tell if we are looking at the whole fern, at one leave of that fern, or at one finger on the leave of the fern. Or perhaps the old saying *big fleas have little fleas upon their backs to bite 'em, little fleas have littler fleas, so ad infinitum.*

It's the idea that 'as above, so below'. The pattern that we see in the human scale being repeated at the atomic scale and at the cosmic scale. What happens within each of us human beings individually also happens to human society. Reiki is 'The One', it helps us appreciate our connectedness to every other aspect of life. 'As above, so below' now being applied between mind, body and soul. Our minds and bodies being reflections of our spiritual self. Fractals and other developments in maths and science increasingly support these ideas.

Chaotic Significance

The oft quoted example of Chaos Theory is that a butterfly flapping its wings in Mexico can cause a hurricane in Honolulu (for example). i.e. Sometimes very small events can have huge consequences. Likewise, sometimes huge events can be totally insignificant. Good evidence that 'there are no rules'. Or rather that the rules of nature are neither logical, predictable nor recognise human definitions of 'normal' or 'reasonable'. Science is now beginning to model some chaotic behaviour, but it's often impossible to gather all the necessary information. Nearly always there are factors which are important which we are not aware of. Not *consciously* aware of that it. This is where Reiki comes in. Whilst we might not be able to see the full picture with logic, with intuition we can. Reiki make us aware of all the relevant factors in a given situation and thus guides us to a more realistic assessment of what we need to do. An example might be that we need to go out but rain is forecast. Do we trust the TV forecast or go out when our intuition tells us to? How often is the formal prediction wrong? What our 'bones' tell us might be more dependable to avoid a soaking.

A Reason for All Things

Whatever happens, or doesn't happen in our lives, they'll be a pretty good reason for it . . somewhere. The world around us, and events we find ourselves part of, reflect our mind and inner needs. But we are part of a far, far, bigger picture. One action of ours *could* affect the future of the world - e.g. a letter that finally decides a particular official to throw his weight behind a particular campaign which results in a prisoner being freed or . . . Or, one decision or event the other side of the world *could* determine what we do next week - e.g. a prominent speaker could fall ill or have an accident and we're called in as a stand-in and happen to be heard by a TV producer who . . .

Our feeble, conscious, human minds cannot possibly know all the things that are linked to our thoughts and deeds. So let's stop trying. The Universe, in contrast, *does* know everything. Our guardian angel knows that somewhere, someone, is about to make a purchase that will enable a second person to go somewhere which . . . which will bring a cheque to us just before the bank starts to complain. Faith . . . in life itself. But why is trusting it so hard? Because of all the habits that we humans have picked up since becoming 'civilised' and 'developed': having to be in control, feeling the need to know the future, and so on.

One of the most difficult lessons on this spiritual path is to accept uncertainty. To *know* that there is a reason for all things . . . but also to accept that often we're not meant to know it! SO often our inner voice tells us to do, or not do something, without telling us why. We know we *have* to go to a given meeting, for example, but no logic can explain why. Even at the meeting, with little to inspire in it, we begin to question our decision. Perhaps we meet one or two reasonably interesting people, then go home. It is not until a few weeks (or months . . . or years!) later that the reason for our attendance becomes clear - when a friend of somebody we met invites us to an event at which we meet our future partner . . . for example.

There *is* a reason for all things. Have faith. All will become clear eventually . . . if it needs to.

Experiential Proof

A major shift in recent years in the scientific community has been the recognition as to how we, as observers and experimenters, affect the projects we're working on. At the atomic level the effect is without question - an atom is either in one place or another depending on whether or not we are measuring it! It seems reasonable, since 'as above so below', that similar effects occur at the level of human society. The implication too is that the results of a scientific experiment may vary depending on what we're thinking. i.e. the physical world is not separate from our thoughts.

Related to this shift in awareness is the acknowledgement that experimental proof is only one way of establishing something as fact. A growing number now accept that if enough people experience a given phenomenon, even if it can't be repeated in a laboratory, then there must be something happening: if enough people have psychic abilities, for example, then there must be something in it.

Consciousness

Discussions of the nature of consciousness and trials of healing all help too to persuade scientists to look beyond their theories and to face a greater reality. As we explore what consciousness is, so we become more aware.

For those keen to pursue such topics, I'd recommend you join *The Scientific and Medical Network,* an international group of scientists (and others) whose mission is "To deepen understanding in science, medicine and education by fostering both rational and intuitive insights".

Manana

Another topic coming in for new thoughts, is time. No longer must we assume that time is linear. Time travel, even according to Einstein, is possible. There *is* a state in which time has no meaning, where all time is one, where past, present and future co-exist. This is the state that we can reach with Reiki. Murry Hope, in "Time - the Ultimate Energy" puts it quite clearly - Time *is* the Ultimate Energy. Or, if you like, Reiki is Time.

The practical implication of this is that any attempts by us to do things when we want them done is wasted effort. The universe has its timing - part of the Divine Order. By tuning into the 'natural order of things', we'll find that sometimes time seems to speed by and at other times it ambles, steadily. Just as a river sometimes rushes and sometimes trickles. The Spanish have a word to describe it - Manana. Literally it means "tomorrow", but not in practice! It wasn't until I spent time in Spain, watching the world go by, that I understood what it means. It's not a case of 'sometime, never' but 'as and when the time is right'. In many rural communities you'll find the same approach to life. Humans accepting that time and tide wait for no man. Scientists too are beginning to see the realities of time. Reiki helps us to experience it.

27 - Practical uses

Whilst the use of Reiki Healing at First Degree Level is restricted to times and places you can put your hands in contact with, or at least close to, the subject; there is no such restriction with Second Degree. With the symbols as tools, Reiki energy can be focused to *any* situation, in any place in past, present or future. The idea is simple - picture the situation in your mind then overlay the symbols or otherwise 'connect' to the Universe. As we clear our minds of our preconceived ideas of what that situation is about, so we become open to the wider picture. Reiki puts things into perspective. It enables us to see difficulties as opportunities, problems as worthwhile challenges, etc, etc. For example:

We find ourselves getting angry because someone who promised to contact us hasn't done so. We picture that person and direct Reiki to our anger . . . *not* to them! It's our emotion and the situation that caused it that we're focusing on . . . others involved may well be innocent bystanders. In this situation, it may just be that this other person is genuinely busy and we're being impatient. If that is so, our Reiki 'treatment' will help us to calm down and allow others to contact us when they're ready . . . when the time is right. It might just happen that whilst we're waiting for their call that we receive some other information that either makes the initial contact unnecessary or changes what we need to say. Perhaps we were going to ask them for a lift . . . and we're told in the meantime that our meetings had been cancelled. Perhaps in not calling us they knew something that we didn't.

Mental Blocks

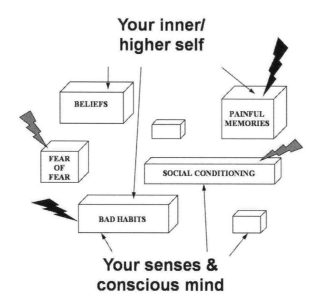

Zap away your mental blocks
- with Reiki

Freedom

Most such examples boil down to us facing our past, letting go of our conditioning and otherwise freeing our minds of habits, beliefs and negative thoughts . . . and eventually of thoughts all-together. After some years of practice, during which we'll have to work though all sorts of grief and resentments, fears and anger, (etc.), the Reiki will be helping to reprogram how our mind works. Gradually it will be able to respond naturally to the here and now . . . instead of reacting emotionally.

To have a mind free of thoughts can feel very strange. Empty. We're so unused to a clear thinking mind that, if we're not careful, we invent new unreal things to think about. Here again the Reiki can help us. Focus love and light into the emptiness . . . and we'll see that emptiness = freedom! In fact this empty mind is just what we've been working towards. *Now* our minds can be open channels for the wisdom and power of the divine. Now we can hear our inner voice - not the usual logic or reactionary.

Who's in Charge?

Try this exercise to identify who *really* makes your better decisions:

Picture a time when you've just made a major change in your life. Maybe got engaged or changed job, moved house, etc. Choose a time when you felt really good afterwards. Picture the situation and your feeling of having no doubts, of knowing this was your best ever decision.

Now go back a few hours or days to when you actually decided this was what you were going to do. Be back in that actual moment of truth. Probably you just KNEW you had to take this step. Sense that feeling of inner calm and certainty. When we follow the voice of our higher self there is a peace and tranquillity surrounding us . . . we have the guidance of angels.

Responsibility

Whilst writing this book a friend pointed out to me the true meaning of 'responsibility' - the ability to respond to the here and now. Think about it. Consider those individuals who we *do* consider to be responsible parents, responsible drivers, responsible children. A responsible person accepts that what happens to them and their lives is up to them. They know it is what they say, do and think that makes the difference.

It is how we act in the moment that determines whether accidents happen, whether we later feel guilty, etc. Responsibility is not about blindly following some set of rules or expectations - not about apportioning blame. Reiki gives us the courage and wisdom to respond honestly and openly to the here and now. By using Reiki when a tricky situation emerges we connect ourselves to the broader truth of the matter and 'go with the flow'. We respond naturally, for the greater good.

A Reiki I student of mine provided an excellent example: *M was driving along, taking due care and attention, when a vehicle was driven out of a side street right across his path. There was no time to avoid him. He responded by braking firmly but not harshly. His higher self took over. His car somehow managed to skid around the car in his path, avoid on-coming traffic and end up heading in the right direction.* A miracle? A very good bit of driving? It was indeed something a trained rally driver would have done - this friend is no rally driver. But the Universe is. All M had to do was to respond to the situation with faith. The alternative? To react with anger and/or fear. Had he done this, he might not be alive today.

OK, you might say he allowed instinct to take over. It was an unconscious act. Maybe, but it illustrates that our unconscious (or perhaps our subconscious or super-conscious) has abilities far beyond our logical conscious mind - it is this higher self that we need to connect into to be truly responsible. The more clear our mind is of conscious doubts and worries the quicker will our higher self come into play and do what has to be done. Watch any of the TV programmes about the emergency services or amazing rescues and we see that the human ability to escape death can be stunning. Having been the victim, then the miracle, those who survive such brushes with death often have a very different idea about responsibility. They *know* that they are able to respond, somehow, to anything . . . and that their guardian angel is part of the equation.

Focusing In

There is often a temptation, when becoming a being of light, to always want to shine your light into the world so that others can see it and benefit. Often we do in deed need to do this. Many of us *are* beacons, our role is to show others the way, to spread a bit of love and light. *But not all the time.* Our own path can be very hard going.

Facing our own past and working through our own issues can be very hard work. Sometimes we need all the light and energy we're able to channel at that time for our own needs. This is the bible story: remove the beam from your own eye before you try to remove the splinter in your brother's. We cannot help others when we ourselves are in real need. But when we are used to giving to others all the time, how can we put ourselves first?

We need to focus our energy within rather than without. Thus, instead of looking around us, seeing suffering and sending love to it, we instead need to recognise our own needs. Shut our eyes, send love to our self. After Reiki II, this is most easily done with the symbols . . . instead of using the symbols to throw Reiki, love, light, over and to those around us, we throw it around ourselves. We wrap ourselves in love so that our own healing process is given the energy it needs.

I had a good example of this a few years ago. I was in the midst of a healing crisis, facing up to some reality about the competitive nature of much of society. It was tough going and meant accepting that my rosy view of the world was only part of the story. At this time I had to go into the local town. Having no car I had to go by bus. As usual when travelling I found myself looking around me, connecting to whoever and whatever I saw. The roads, busy with commerce, did nothing to raise my spirits. It was, on that occasion, too much for me to cope with. The solution was to focus in on myself. So with eyes closed I drew (in my mind) the Reiki symbols on, in and around me. Slowly I began to feel myself again. Safe and secure with my own light. OK, it wasn't as bright as usual, it wasn't shining out to others. But this meant that those in need were not being drawn to me. I was left alone to look after myself. And, in this protected place, the Universe ensured that I wasn't hit with new challenges that I had no energy to deal with. The trip went very smoothly, all my tasks completed with minimal effort . . . my energy being focused to where it was most needed on that day . . . my own inner healing.

Protected by Reiki

The above situation also provides an answer to those who ask about Reiki and protection. Some people look for a shield from negative energies. Reiki can certainly be used to help us feel safe in challenging or even threatening situations, but to see it is a protective shield can give the wrong impression. Shields can isolate us, barriers can cut us off from the world. To do thus can separate us, can encourage denials of the world around. Reiki is about facing situations and learning to handle them, not about putting up barriers between us and things we don't like.

Having said that, things *do* get too much and at times we do feel in need of protection. The solution is to use Reiki with symbols to focus the healing energy within, so that we are enveloped in love and light. Any negative energy directed at us will be reflected by our cocoon of love, or neutralised before it can affect us.

Negative Forces?

Reiki, the Universal Life Force Energy, just IS. It is neither 'negative' nor 'positive', it embraces all poles, all categories that we might like to label it (or specific aspects of it) with. But within this all embracing energy are there separate, 'evil' forces at work? By defining them as 'separate' we immediately identify them as forces not in alignment with the greater good, entities that seek to further their own ends without regard for others; beings that consider themselves apart from The Oneness. There is no doubt that many humans could be so labelled, so from that respect they could be considered 'evil'. Likewise it seems reasonable to assume that entities other than humans might adopt a same, separate, approach to their lives.

The question is thus whether these 'negative' people (or beings) pose us any threat. Obviously there are no rules. At times we will need to steer clear of them, at others we'll be able to face them with impunity. The point about 'separate' entities is just that - they have isolated themselves, they are disconnected from others. This leaves THEM weak and vulnerable. Those, 'connected' to The Oneness (as when 'in' Reiki), always have its unlimited resources as protection.

There is one force that might be considered 'negative' that is fairly universal: entropy. The gradual, but persistent, tendency of things with order to disintegrate into chaos. It applies to all material things in our world: wood rots, iron rusts, our bodies decay, even mountains crumble given sufficient time. We can't stop it. But by being aware of it, we can work with the process and allow it to happen as it has to. Trying to stop it is an impossible, or at least never ending, process . . . as anyone who's tried to protect a sand-castle against an incoming tide will tell you! Whilst Reiki might sometimes help to delay the inevitable, more usually it encourages us to accept it.

Entropy, the ageing process, is a challenge for us in this life. But it relates only to the physical world . . . and to our emotions and mental constructs. Anything that we, or nature, creates is likely to be broken apart again sooner or later. It's all part of the cycle of life. Reiki, particularly at second degree, enables us to see this cycle without getting caught up in it . . . to rise above . . . and fly through life.

28 - Onwards & upwards?

OK, so you've done second degree Reiki and feel ready to move on. Or you've been training in other healing arts and wonder if Reiki is for you. Is this the right thing to do? *Only YOU know the answer to that!* Whilst keeping my students informed of higher level courses, I rarely try to persuade them to move on. We each progress along our own path in our own time. Often I will hear nothing from a student for months or years then suddenly they'll reappear and be keen to take the next step. This is maybe how it should be . . . except that there are no rules.

Some 'authorities' suggest minimum times between each of the levels of Reiki training. Whilst agreeing that all students need *some* time to absorb the experience, to practice and to assimilate it, I find the placing of any firm durations to be unreal . . . for we are all different. Those who did Reiki I and II together or in quick succession may need considerable time to integrate all the experiences before they are ready to move on. Or they may already have been so open to the energy, as natural healers or psychics for example, that Reiki attunements represent only a small incremental step on their path. If it doubt, talk to your chosen Master (see Chapter 30) . . . you don't have to use the same Master at all levels!

Retakes

Like any other subject, it's possible to retake a Reiki course . . . at any level . . . either with the same or a different tutor. As is explained in the section on attunements (Chapter 14), there are no absolutes in Reiki. Although (most) Reiki teachers have (fairly) set procedures for attunements at First Degree, Second Degree and Masters level, this doesn't make them fixed events. On the contrary.

It does no harm at all to repeat a given level of training and have extra attunements . . . if that's what you feel is right for you.

Some of the reasons you might feel such 'retakes' to be necessary are:

* You're not happy with your original tutor - that doesn't mean they're no good, just that they weren't right for you at that time

* You just want to experience another way of looking at it - a good reason! As we've seen, Reiki is very personal; two different Reiki teachers could, together, help you see what Reiki means for YOU.

* You're not ready to move on. i.e. you know you need some more training, but are not ready to move to the next level. This is not a sign of failure by you or your original instructor. Getting onto the Reiki Route (i.e. Reiki as a conscious path to self & spiritual growth) often takes a significant shift in how we see the world. To make changes in our life we might need a significant boost in our energy levels. On the first course we might begin to feel the possibilities, on the second we might gain the inner strength to actually pursue the Reiki Route once the course has finished.

Attunements and training in Reiki are part of our on-going personal development. We each do our best. Sometimes we need to repeat certain lessons in order to fully learn what we need to learn and to assimilate it into our lives. Whatever you need to do is right for you.

Not ready?

To surrender is a big step, and paths to enlightenment mean, for most of us, surrendering. Although it tends to happen a bit at a time, parts of us will decide that this isn't a step we're ready to take. How do we know when we're ready? *When the inner voice wins over any other voice!*

What often gets in the way, are voices of our old selves and our current self deciding who's who. i.e. The mental processing of coming to terms with our past. Whilst we're still angry about things that have happened in the past (like being battered or pushed into a relationship or career), we're unlikely to be able to surrender to the here and now.

To surrender is particularly difficult for those who have spent their life at the beck and call of others. It seems that many who feel they have been used or squashed by parents, bosses or partners need to assert themselves first. Indeed, maybe we all need to have 'found ourselves' before we are ready to immerse ourselves in The One. How can we surrender until we know who and what it is we are giving up?

Another way of looking at it would be to say that we cannot give that which we haven't got. If we don't feel in control of our lives, how can we give that control back to the Universe?

The two processes, becoming our assertive, true, self and surrendering to the Universe may run in parallel for some of us, but often we need a considerable time on our own, finding a peace within ourselves, before we are ready to merge with others. This could explain why so many are choosing to live alone at present. We *need* that time and space to face our past and tease out the real us . . . this may not be possible with others around. Here Reiki really comes into its own - it enables us to feel loved even when we have nobody physically with us.

At the time of first drafting this book and for 12 years previously, I lived alone. It's thus not possible for me to suggest, from first hand experience, how to combine Reiki with a family life . . . that may be the subject of a future book. However, living alone has been essential in giving me the confidence to be me. Without the constant demands of others I have been able, with Reiki's help, to focus on the needs of this particular mind/body, to free myself from its (self-imposed) restrictions

The following is the sort of exercise I might do if beginning to feel a little lonely:

You are Not Alone

Place one hand over your heart and the other on your stomach or throat (whichever feels comfortable). Feel the heart beat and focus

your attention on the rhythm of your blood flow. Know that this is just one rhythm amongst many in life - your breathing, the days and nights, the seasons. All automatic. Rising and falling, in and out. The natural flow of life. Within and around us, sustaining us, nurturing us, loving us. Sense it, be with it . . . for as long as you need.

Say to yourself "I love you . . . ", including your own name in the sentence. And again, with feeling. Mean it. "I love YOU". It doesn't matter when there is nobody around for us to love, or nobody to love us . . . we can love ourselves. We are both lover and loved. Give yourself a hug. Tell yourself "Well done" for putting yourself first. All the lovely thoughts and feelings that you might send or give to someone special, lavish on yourself. Here and Now YOU are that someone special. You are healing yourself and in doing so healing your life . . . including all relationships in it. No one can BE alone.

"It didn't work"

Some people don't get on with Reiki. They don't get the results they'd like through using it. Maybe it isn't the path, technique (or whatever) for them. Or maybe they're not ready for it. I'd suggest the following as relevant factors in such situations:

* Expectations are too high. Whilst Reiki *can* bring miracles about, it rarely does so to order. Who are we to decide what should happen as a result of a Reiki treatment or attunement? - see Chapter 13 on intent.

* We're not prepared to do our bit. Similar to the above really. i.e. Reiki works in its own way in its own time, but we have to demonstrate our commitment to the process. For Reiki to do its 'best' we often need to show the Universe that we're prepared to make sacrifices.

i.e. "God helps those that help themselves". If, for example, our illness results from a bad habit (lack or breath due to smoking, for example) we can't really expect Reiki to restore our full breathing ability until we're willing to kick the smoking habit! Reiki is very good at pointing out the truth to us . . . there are rarely short cuts, even with Reiki. It will help us face and deal with bad habits, it will enable us to throw the skeletons out of our cupboards, but only *we* can do the sorting out.

Having said that, Reiki might work where other therapies or approaches have failed . . . just because it helps us face reality. It might also happen that some other technique might bring about a miraculous recovery where Reiki hadn't had the desired results . . . at least at the time. What healing processes had it set in motion though?

If you want to be cured without any effort then Reiki, at least as presented here, isn't for you. Having said that, there are many healers (Reiki or otherwise) who see their role as healings others. Each to their own path. If the Universe considers you have already learnt your lessons, then you will receive the healing you need. Enjoy it and be thankful.

REIKI MASTERS: ALL DIMENSIONS

29 - How to become One

"Be prepared for anything but expect nothing" is perhaps a good motto for an aspiring Master. As we face our angers and fears we become aware just how conditioned we are to being in control of our life . . . and thus that our disappointments arise from our expectations. By tuning into 'all pasts, all presents and all possible futures', we prepare ourselves for *all* eventualities. Yes, our dreams may still be possible but we now see them in perspective, with all their implications. We also see the 'worst' that can happen . . . and all the other unlimited range of possibilities. We begin to see that nothing is certain but anything is possible.

Even in the conventional world of business, it is being accepted that flexibility is key. Those who are able to cope with change are the ones that will survive. Or, as I like to put it: *Welcome uncertainty into your life, it enables the angels to perform miracles.* i.e. the more open we are to new possibilities, the more likely is it that wonderful things will happen. Conversely, if we insist on maintaining the status quo or pursuing our limited pre-chosen path, then we have to 'suffer the consequences'.

There is a song in the Folk Opera "Larkrise to Candelford" which fits how I often feel when accepting all this. When the heart starts thumping, when you *know* there's so much you *could* be doing to improve your lot, when you need some courage:

Reiki - Without Rules

Dare to be a Daniel, dare to walk alone
Dare to have a purpose true, dare to make it known

and/or give yourself a Reiki treatment. One trick is to learn to tell the difference between butterflies in the stomach . . . adrenaline urging you to 'just do it' and fear caused by unrealistic expectations. *Put your hands on your stomach and heart, tune into the feelings. Think peace and calm. Allow the healing light to pervade the anxiety. What's left? Is there an inner confidence urging to get on and do what has to be done? If so, do it.* If not, then it's not right, so don't!

A Leap of Faith

Perhaps what's needed most as we let go of our attachment to worldly possessions and ideas, is faith. Not faith in anything or anybody, but in life itself, in The Universe. After all, does a butterfly need a blue-print to change from being a caterpillar? Do shrubs and trees need to be told to produce fruit? No, they just do it. All too often our brains interfere with the natural processes that would better satisfy our needs.

So, becoming a Master is about *allowing* our true self to take control. Doing what we *have* to do. A good example was when, after 17 years in the electronics industry I knew I had to 'move on'. I was no longer getting any satisfaction from the job. I looked at various options but nothing seemed right . . . until I had the opportunity to learn to teach Reiki. It was not long (days rather than months) before I had handed in my notice! When my engineering colleagues heard what I was doing they said "That's very brave"; to which my response was "It's an act of faith" . . . or rather, a *leap* of faith. The challenges since then have been huge, the learning curves steep . . . but the satisfaction immeasurable. The times of absolute bliss more frequent and long lasting. I hear similar stories from others on the Reiki (and other similar) paths . . . and, I'm glad to say, often from my students. They too seem to appreciate the freedom to live without rules.

Where is heaven?

With each 'letting go' we free ourselves from another bit of conditioning. The peeling away the layers of an onion being a good analogy - particularly as both activities often produce copious tears.

Another analogy might be the Russian Dolls - one within another. Thus, the outer layer might represent particular thoughts and feelings related to a relationship. The next layer might be concerned with blocks from childhood. The third layer might be our experiences and beliefs on religion. The next might be doubts and worries about money. At times it will feel that there is no end to the layers of unreal thoughts that we've been carrying around with us - or one layer will keep coming back to haunt us. Decades of conditioning is hard work to overcome.

So IS there a tiny Russian Doll underneath all this? Maybe. Maybe a time does come when we have totally cleared our mind. When we become a true channel for God's love and light. What are the indicators for such a state:

* Living totally in the here and now - no thoughts at all about what has happened or might happen . . . unless there is a genuine need to do so.

* No judgements about things around us. Instead a natural discernment on what to get involved in and what to stay detached from.

* When involved in the human world we do so fully, in mind, body and soul. Our senses are heightened, our energy strong and our wisdom flows.

* When in detached mode we're able to stay in a 'place' of inner peace.

Note that 'being' implies no particular set of values and ways of living - other than allowing ourselves to be channels through which the Universe operates. There are no rules.

Heaven is a state of mind, not a person or place. It is the ability to respond naturally to the here and now

Reiki - Without Rules

Who am I?

During the early days on my conscious path to finding the real me, I gave up asking "Who am I?" and instead asked "What am I?". After a while I(!) became comfortable with the idea of being a spiritual being, a being of light, an essence. The next tricky question was to accept that this new 'I', whilst being part of the greater One, was also a unique entity. Each of us has a specific soul purpose, each human being has characteristics that are his or hers only . . . and yet we are not separate. A typical contradiction! The truth is that both are true . . . we are unique *and* we are an inseparable part of the greater being that is life itself . . . like a drop in the ocean, like a leaf on a tree. One cannot exist without the other. If each leaf were exactly the same, it wouldn't be much of a tree.

Star Trek Deep Space Nine gives us a good visual image of this, with Odo the changeling. This being can 'shape-shift', change his form to appear as anything else. On his home land his 'people' form a 'sea', each unique changeling becomes just a drop in their ocean . . . like the primordial soup from which we all came.

Because society is so geared to humans being separate individuals, all this can be hard to accept, but to go 'home' we have to be willing and able to be reabsorbed into the cosmic jelly of life. Being able to retain our uniqueness makes this much easier. The following exercise may help. It can start as a visualisation or be an actual walk.

The I that is 1

You are walking alone in a peaceful, natural, place. Go wherever you feel most at home. Allow the scene to fill your senses. Perhaps it is on a beach just as the sun is setting, the waves lapping on the shore. Or perhaps you are in a wood or forest. Feel the dead leaves beneath your feet, listen to the songs of birds and rustling of the branches around you. Look around and soak in the whole picture. All around there is life, in the wind, in the birds, in any animals that you can see or know to be hidden from view. Allow your attention to focus on one aspect of the picture . . . something that's moving . . .

perhaps its a leaf or a wave. Watch it change its position, up and down, up and down. Always moving, but never the same movement twice. Allow your mind to ebb and flow with the tide as one drop of water within the surf . . . or to rise up and down with the branch of a tree as one leaf amongst hundreds. Feel that you are unique, a very special living thing . . . and at the same time you are lost in the greater picture. Without you there could be nothing or everything. You are distinct AND an integral part of life.

Master Training

But what's all this got to do with training to be a Reiki Master? Hopefully, *everything*! Most Reiki Master classes will give you another symbol. Classes for Reiki Master Teachers will show you how to attune others. But these are not ends in themselves. We take training to become a Reiki Master because it is a necessary step on our personal spiritual journey. Unless we are conscious of the decision in these terms, then maybe we're not really ready for this step,

Having said that, every Reiki Master reached that level in their own way in their own time - and will teach accordingly. Every Reiki Master is different as are every student's needs. Choosing the right combination is part of the process of becoming a true Master.

THE Master

During one particular Reiki I class one of my students referred to me, on a number of occasions as 'The Reiki Master'. Not 'A master', but 'The Master'. It made me gulp a bit. At around the same time I was finding that often when I started to speak, all eyes would look my way. It's easy to see how an unnatural sense of self importance might result from being a Reiki Master.

The reality of course is that 'The Master' is God him/her self . . . and thus our inner/higher self. The 'I that is 1' IS The Master . . . it does, after all, know everything! That others identify this wisdom as being present within us is a useful sign that we *have* been able to suspend our ego self . . . we have to accept that we ARE blessed with divine authority and the greatest wisdom. As and when we need it. The rest of the time we're nothing, nobody. Our view is worthless. We are no more significant than an ant in the garden. Maybe less so. We are 'nothing yet all'. The Master IS the greatest of the great AND the lowest of the low.

There are few humans who come anywhere near achieving this range of being. Gandhi was perhaps a good example, and someone to aspire to. SO humble, so insignificant in many ways yet with the inner strength and authority to make a real difference in and to his society.

But Gandhi was Gandhi. You are you and I am me. We're not all here to challenge imperialism or to lead a nation. But we DO all have a role to play in society. And with Reiki we can become a Master of that particular role - be it teaching Reiki in a particular area or to a given group of students, or nursing the terminally ill, or creating works or art . . . or growing the best organic veg in our part of the world.

30 - How to choose one

How do you choose the right Reiki Master for you? *You let it happen!* You might not even be lead to Reiki - you might be lead to use music or dance as your path to enlightenment. You might not even need to actually *do* anything - in the sense of going on any course. Your path might be 'just' to live your life along the lines you're already living it. In this case the 'Masters' who teach you might be your children, or neighbours' pets, or a 'chance' meeting with a visiting guru . . . or pretty much anything or everything that comes across your path. The Universe is our teacher and Master . . . but from time to time it'll choose to let a human 'Master' do the work.

But lets say you feel drawn to Reiki and would like learn it for your own benefit. How do you find the right Reiki Master Teacher for you? At the time of writing there is no one all-embracing listing of Reiki teachers. So other than doing a search on the Internet or looking in the yellow pages or local directories, how do you go about making the connection?

Just let it happen. Pose the question in your mind, pray for guidance . . . and keep your eyes and ears open. If it's meant to be, you'll just happen across an advert for a course, see a list of Evening Classes or be introduced to someone who knows someone.

Similarly with books. The one for you is the one that jumps off the shelf in front of you. If it feels right, it is. At least for that day.

The path to enlightenment is one through rapidly changing countryside. The key book yesterday is now ready to be passed to another. The guy who inspired you last year may have nothing more to teach you. Follow your nose and you'll find whoever or whatever you need to guide you . . . if anybody: Maybe you already have the only guide you need . . . the guide within you. He/she is probably chuckling quietly to itself even as you read this.

All in One?

Some Reiki teachers offer Reiki I and Reiki II or even I, II and Masters all in one 2 or 3 day course. That is their choice. If this feels right for you, then go for it. My experience in teaching Reiki would however suggest that Reiki is like a good Port - it's too good to hurry. My previous occupation in Quality Assurance would also sound a note of caution - you pays your money and you takes your choice. As we've discussed (Chapter 17 - The $10,000 Question) straight cost isn't the only issue here, but logic, intuition and experience tend to agree that if you try to do something too quickly and/or too cheaply the chances are that something will be missing. But what?

It's only my opinion of course, but combining First and Second degree in a single training course risks significant overload at a number of levels:

* Embodiment. As Reiki is self regulating it's unlikely that we can over-do attunements. However, it does take real time - like days, weeks, months even years, to assimilate a Reiki attunement. For many it can be a whole new experience and thus require considerable adjustments (e.g. in attitudes and ways of thinking) before we've fully absorbed one set of attunements.

* Information Saturation. A comprehensive course for Reiki I and II contains not just the attunements but background information on how Reiki relates to life. There is a lot to teach . . . and to learn. Maybe it can all be packed into two full days . . . but this would be a bit like teaching the works of Shakespeare in a weekend. Intense to the point of being too concentrated to be digestible.

Some would argue that only the attunement is necessary. It might be for some. My experience is that most of us have enquiring minds that need some context for the attunement. i.e. we need at least *some* intellectual appreciation of what Reiki is and how it can be used. This will be different for each of us . . . which is not only an argument for longer courses but also for smaller numbers of students.

In my years teaching I have had only a few students who have been ready, willing and able to progress from First to Second degree in under a couple of months. These were exceptional students. Individuals who were already practised spiritual healers or had already spent much time working on their own self development, or well practised in Buddhism. The others (95%+ of them) all needed many months or years to practice hands-on Reiki and to assimilate the basic Reiki experience before they were ready to move on.

To do Reiki II at the same time as Reiki I is a bit like taking an advanced driving test at the same time as taking your normal driving test. OK, if you've been driving professionally for many years, you may pass both . . . but only if you truly are a natural and experienced driver.

Combining Reiki I and II in a single course is consistent with our times. But is that because we're so conditioned to expect things now, now, now . . . or because we are genuinely ready, willing and able to assimilate two mind-blowing experiences at the same time?

The same points apply equally to Reiki Masters courses. Rush them or rush into them and you risk missing out on some of the depth and breadth that is possible with Reiki. As usual with Reiki however, the opposite argument may be applicable to others: if you feel drawn to take Reiki Masters, then *just do it!* If the time is right, money and teachers will appear - 'things' will only get in the way if they need to . . . if you're *not* ready.

So, I'm in favour of spreading out Reiki training but not in favour of minimum times between levels. Just as a high price is no guarantee of a high quality service, so many months of elapsed time is no guarantee that someone has assimilated a level of Reiki sufficiently. There are no rules. We are all different. Any decent Master will encourage his student to ask themselves, in truth, whether they are ready to move on. Both will *know* when the time is right.

Controlling Influence

Whilst some Reiki Masters may see themselves as gurus and be happy for their students to 'follow' them, that isn't how I see the

Reiki Master - Student relationship. There is a fine line to be trod between encouraging a student and steering them. It raises the whole question of control:

If we look around us we see a spread between two extremes when it comes to being in control. At one end we have The Controller. The individual who is in control of everything . . . or thinks he is. His life is governed by diaries and timetables, his staff and family do what he wants 'or else' . . . and he's probably even got a regimented garden.

At the other end of the spectrum we have The Controlled. The door-mat, the set-upon individual who does what they're told by parent, partner, boss, advertisers, etc. Whereas The Controller has a grossly inflated view of 'self', The Controlled has an almost non-existent view of who and what they are.

So where does a Reiki Master, or any other aware, enlightened being, fit into this spectrum? They span it. A true Master is willing and able to be a controller, or controlled, *depending on circumstances.* At times a Master *knows* that he must allow others to have their way. (S)he will do so with humility, with respect, happy to take a subservient role as and when required.

At other times, perhaps when the situation required a leader, a true Master asserts the divine authority they have vested in them. They do so not with any personal motive except that of doing what they have to do. Of fulfilling their soul purpose.

A true master has confidence in himself without being cocky, (s)he leads by example and through commanding respect . . . by showing respect. A true master knows that they are not in control. They know that the Universe just IS, that 'what will be will be'. 'Control' is unreal, a concept of human invention.

Except . . . Of course, there are no rules, so even this 'rule' has an exception. The control that has some reality about it, is *self* control. A true master has self control in abundance - the ability to master their own thoughts and feelings so that they can respond truly to the here and now. When our thoughts and feelings are natural, untainted by memories and dreams, when our mind is a clear channel for divine wisdom and love, *then* we are in control of our lives . . . or rather we *are* our lives.

Just another way?

So Reiki is just another way of becoming our true selves? *Exactly!* It's no more special and no less special than any other path we might tread or technique we might use to help us see who and what we really are. Each path is valid for those who are drawn to it. . . . and each variant of Reiki is valid for those pursuing it. How can any one path, technique, method (or therapy for that matter) be any better than any other? They all have their differences and so cannot be compared. At times one line of Reiki, one philosophical school or a particular therapy will feel *right* for us. That doesn't make it 'better' or the only path of truth! Just what we need at that moment. Judging paths, therapies, etc. achieves nothing. The only relevant question is 'is this path/method/therapist/teacher right for *me now?'*. If the answer seems to be "No", move on - without resentment, if "Yes", throw yourself into the technique with mind, body and soul.

That's what matters. Not which technique we adopt to assist our spiritual growth in life, but that we apply ourselves to it - fully. Very little will 'work' if we don't do our bit. God helps those who help themselves. I remember a story told by Bernard Miles (later Sir Bernard Miles) which my parents had on a 78rpm record:

The vicar was walking around his village when he noticed that one garden that had been derelict & growing wild was now looking beautiful. He spoke to the man who was tending the plot "It's wonderful what God can do in the garden with a bit of help". To which the gardener replied "Yes, but you should have seen it when he had it to himself".

Bringing heaven to earth is joint effort. We have to show our commitment, reach out to the Universe and allow ourselves to go with its flow. *Then* we'll be provided with what we need.

The commitment required isn't to any particular path but to life itself . . .and to the Universe, as the following story illustrates:

R was a therapist with a broad range of skills. She'd spent many years learning new techniques which she practised very professionally often with some success. Her treatment room was covered with certificates - Aromatherapy, Reflexology, Reiki, Kinesiology, Bach Flower Remedies, Karuna, etc, etc. In each she was technically proficient and her manner with clients was supportive and caring . . . hence her success. However, in herself R often felt unhappy, discontent, unfulfilled. Her therapies were her life, but only in a mechanical sense. They were used on her clients but rarely on herself. They were still a series of therapies, not an integrated, holistic approach to life by which she lived. That is not to judge R. This approach was her choice . . . and what she (and her clients at the time) needed. But from the outside it was clear to see that R had not entered into Reiki (or any other techniques) with her *whole* mind, body and soul.

No technique or path will make any significant impact on our lives until we let it become part of us, until we identify it's spirit and let our ourselves live it as part of our day-to-day life. i.e.

* Physically - Practice the method on ourselves as and when we need it - throughout each day. We cannot heal ourselves if we don't treat ourselves and give *this* mind/body the love and attention it deserves.

* Mentally - our rational minds need to be comfortable with whatever technique we adopt. So let it ask its question and do your best to give it some answers. Any decent teacher of any philosophy or healing technique will welcome searching questions. Challenge your Master, challenge your own perceptions of 'life the universe and everything' and your mind will begin to change.

* Spiritually - the whole point is to bring out our spiritual essence, to allow our soul to 'come out' into the real world. This inner part of us is thus going to be most supportive of those healing methods and philosophies which enable *it* to feel alive. Reiki connects our mind/body self to our spiritual self . . . *when we allow it to.* When we allow this 'coming out', our heart and soul will sing with joy . . . we are beginning to truly live again.

Reiki - Without Rules

What often happens in courses is that we accept what we're told. Because that's what we're conditioned to do. The truth is that no matter how famous a guru, how respected a Master, (or how much you've paid for your training), what you're told may not be right for you. We are all different. Having had different upbringings and being in this world for different purposes, we *will* have a different perspective on certain aspects of life. A true Master will be aware of your needs and might propose a new insight *but only YOU know YOUR truth.*

Perhaps my truths, the ideas in this book, are too challenging? Quite likely! In which case, put this book aside and pick it up again in a few months or years time. You'll know when you *are* ready.

From this comes a few tips in identifying a decent teacher of Reiki - or for that matter any other subject:

A good teacher:

* Encourages students to ask questions, even to question his or her wisdom. They know that they are not perfect.

* Listens to *your* ideas and shares your experiences. He/she will be interested in your skills. A true teacher is always willing and able to learn. My own appreciation of different paths has been greatly assisted by my Reiki students who've been adept at Yoga, Nutrition, Tai Chi, etc. By sharing openly we all benefit.

* Do not insist on anything. They encourage you to find a way of seeing and doing things that is right *for you.*

* Set a good example - in their manner, their approach to life. Do they live as you're seeking to live? If not, what are you following them for?

31 - Re-alignment

I've used the term 'reprogramming' a number of times: the idea that as we let Reiki work within us it helps us to change our ways of thinking. The analogy between our brains and computer programs is useful: Gradually we delete our sub-routines (thought processes) for 'worry' and for 'anger' . . . as we realise they cause more harm than good. We are debugging our minds! Removing those programs that were created when we didn't really know what we were doing.

Some people talk of being 're-wired' as they become more aware. As we grow, as spiritual beings, so we 'take our instructions' (on how we behave in life) not from our conditioning but from our higher self. Instead of listening to our memories, we listen to that 'still small voice of calm' which is the God within us. So we are reprogramming, being rewired, or re-aligned. Aligning our thoughts, words and deeds not with what our rational, conditioned, ego, mind wants but with what our soul *knows* we *need* to think, say or do.

For example, we might be having a meal out and feel fairly full, although there's still some food on our plate. On what basis de we decide what to do? For a start, at least during our rewiring process, we'll feel uneasy. We'll be aware that we have a mental conflict. Our memories will recall our parents always telling us to "leave an empty plate". Our logical mind may be saying "You've paid for this, eat it. Waste not, want not". Our conditioning will be throwing all these "shoulds" and "oughts" at us. Our real self, now beginning to assert itself, will be wise to their little games. "There are No Rules" will be 'heard' as our inner self assesses the situation. "What's the reality here? What do you *need* to do?" And so the question as to how we respond, here and now, is decided on what our genuine needs are. Not by how we have always reacted in the past. Maybe we'll remember that it'll be a long time before we'll eat again so *do* empty the plate. Or perhaps our stomach tells us that it *has* had enough and we follow its lead.

Re-wiring

FROM

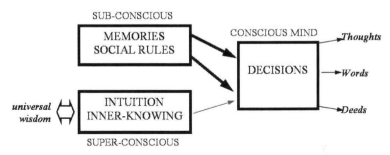

Why we're often in two (or more) minds!

TO

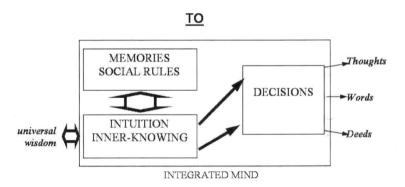

At peace with ourselves and the world

This is what is meant by re-alignment. Doing what is right for us, here, now. Coming into line with our soul purpose. Going with the flow of our soul's progression. It can work at the day-to-day level, as in the above example, or for major life decisions - like relationships and jobs. Is our job helping us to learn what we need to learn in life . . . or merely satisfying our conditioned desire for more money and a bigger house and car? As we become 'true to ourselves' so we stop listening to our old habits or beliefs, or to the bit of us that wants an easy life. We know that to feel fulfilled we have to follow our inner calling.

But that's being selfish? *Is it? Ask yourself where that question came from!* Probably from not being allowed to follow your heart at earlier stages in your life. To follow the guidance of our higher self is not at all the same as always doing what we want. That *is* being selfish - giving no concern about anything or anybody else. Neither are we talking about being self-less: to *always* put other people first can be equally damaging to our inner selves. There is a middle path - being self-*full*: standing up for our needs when that's necessary, helping others when that's required . . . and being able to switch between the two modes as and when we need.

When we are true with our inner self we are fully aware of the implications of what we are doing, maybe not consciously, but it's all taken care of by the Universe. When we act on orders from 'our higher self', that higher self is also everybody else's higher self. It knows what everybody needs. Thus, by satisfying our own true needs we automatically satisfy the needs of anybody else affected by our decision. God knows best because (s)he knows everything. We are realigning our will to God's will.

Free Will

Ah, so we have no free will? *Of course we do!* We can choose to follow God's will or to carry on following our conditioning and ego wants. We can 'go with the divine flow' or insist on doing our own thing. We have the choice to do things *my* way or to listen to our higher selves and live in harmony with the world around us.

My experience is that God, The Universe, genuinely cares for me. I *know* that by following this voice I'll be guided to where I need to be and encouraged to take the lessons I need to learn. And one of those lessons is that the more we fight this flow, the more painful life is. Yes, we suffer as we let go of our past - grief seems to be part of the process, but if we insist on ignoring the signs, then the path gets far tougher.

Having said that, this whole realignment process can be hard, often painful work. We are, after all, often changing the habits of a life-time. If something has been part of us for decades we can't expect it to let go without a fight. So go easy on yourself. By giving ourselves plenty of Reiki treatments we can ease this re-wiring, we can allow the grief (or any other emotions stored from the past) to work itself through our system. Slowly but surely we can feel the baggage lifting from our minds.

Bring the inner child into play. Have fun in the process! Call on the angels to help. One visualisation I particularly like (I think it comes from one of Betty Shine's wonderful books) is of the 'Spring Cleaning Angel':

Picture in your mind an angel with a vacuum cleaner. As she goes around your mind she sucks up all the negative thoughts, throws bad habits into a recycling bin and leaves our minds free and clear.

And allow our creativity in. Perhaps we enjoy singing - so change a few words to a good old song to match our inner processing:

"*Unpack* your troubles from your old kit bag and smile, smile, smile". Our re-alignment can be fun, if that is our intent.

A common feeling during all this undoing, can be of resentment. We can get fed up of being 'told' what to do. We can get angry at folks who seem to be getting away with letting their egos run their lives. This just shows how much our own ego is clinging to its little world. Remind it that by following the divine will, it too will benefit. God is not some separate, dictatorial boss, but part of us, within us. And we are part of God, an integrated part. I've found that the resentment passes, partly with plenty of healing treatments, but also by reassuring the old me that this is all in our best interests. Experiences since starting Reiki all support this. The realignment is thus about accepting that: *Our* Will Be Done. 'Our', the cosmic One. Not the 'Royal We' or the religious 'Thou' but the 'Divine We'. If in doubt, just remember that 'Our Will Be Done'.

Reiki - Without Rules

For a Reason?

Why do we do or not do a given something? *There is only one reason to take a given action - because we HAVE to.* i.e. because that is what our higher self guides us to do. We are here to serve our soul purpose.

That's it. No more, no less. To justify our actions in any way is to allow our rational minds to take control again. Even to analyse our soul purpose and label or categorise it is to descend into the old way of thinking. To BE is to rise above the descriptions and justifications, to detach ourselves from mental strife and just do whatever we have to, from the heart & soul . . . with joy.

Let me use my own growth process as an example:

A few years before I left my job in the electronics industry I was feeling frustrated and wanting to move on. I went on a weekend to play The Transformation Game (TM) with the intent of gaining some guidance on a career move. The advice I received (the TG is good like that!) was that I HAD to stay put. The guidance was clear: my role was to bring spiritual (or at least holistic) values and practices INTO my current area of work. It was not what I wanted to hear, but I'd already learnt that there's no arguing with The Boss (the TG).

I swallowed my impatience and faced up to the job given to me. No sooner had I done so when two wonderful opportunities, within my existing job, came to me. Both enabled me to spread my message and do things that brought a bit of heart and soul into the business. I started to enjoy my job again!

Now, a few years on, my inner guide is again reminding me of my job on earth - to bring holistic and spiritual ideas and practices into 'the mainstream'. I could, from this, decide that this is my Soul Purpose and make such tasks my main aim in life. I know that is not what it's about: writing this book, for example, is but a small part of it.

Looking back at the turn around in my old job, I can see that by accepting my responsibility, I changed the reality. I had to stay where I was to prove (to myself and the universe) that I COULD face the harsher realities of life. Having faced them, having faced the associated fears and frustrations, so the universe allowed me to move on.

So it is now. I'm being urged to take my message out of my classes into 'the wider world', not because my soul purpose is to teach, but because the only way this mind-body is going to grow is to face the conventional world. This path towards unconditional love requires that I accept and love ALL in society. What better way of demonstrating this than by facing the parts of society that in the past have made me squirm?

So we do what we *have* to do. For the sake of our soul's development. And in doing so everybody benefits. Once we have surrendered our separate selves and become part of the One, then concepts such as 'selfless' and 'selfish' have no meaning. All actions are for 'the Greater Good' which includes us, those we help . . . and those who help us, one being the mirror of the other.

That's what I mean by 'there are no rules': to say we do something 'to help others' or 'because it's right' isn't the whole reason for our actions. We do what we do because we have to, because our inner self requires us to, for everybody's benefit. *That's* the reason that matters. To intellectualise our actions is to get attached to beliefs and aims. No matter how worthy our cause, it is still an attachment, a concept of the human mind which could end up getting in the way of our personal soul journey. We may indeed have important work to do for others, but we must be wary of letting it take us over. Our inner self is our only true guide, not a campaign objective - no matter how worthy it might sound.

Again I'll illustrate this with personal experience: *A role I took on some years ago now, was co-ordinator to the local holistic network (Sailing with Spirit). I knew it was an important job and I'd always realised that one of my roles in life is 'catalyst and lubricant' - bringing people together. Thus I got involved and helped get the network going. We were enthusiastic and full of ideas and plans. We allowed these to over-take us and after an initial flurry of*

Reiki - Without Rules

successes we found things not working out as we'd imagined. THAT we saw was the problem! We'd imagined and planned based on a written (or at least verbalised) set of objectives. We'd let specific, human, thoughts blind us from truth. We learnt that our network and magazine has a life of it's own, that we are merely enablers. We also learnt that it was but one part of our Soul Purpose and that the Universe tells us which bit to work on at any given moment. Part of the reason for getting involved in the work was to learn these lessons.

So it is with ANY campaign, hobby or voluntary work we find ourselves part of. Yes we help others, but we are also helping ourselves on *our* soul journey.

We are conditioned, in this society, to be forever judging. Always we have to decide between this belief and that belief, between this team and that team. This is unreal. The truth is that the 'either/or' mentality doesn't fit our emerging spirituality. Now we are experiencing one-ness, an all-inclusive reality. Thus it's not this OR that, it's this AND that. ALL options have some validity for somebody at some time.

In "Iron John" Robert Bly makes some good points about 'opposites'. He suggests that as we find our true self, our real masculine and genuine feminine within, so we learn to accept the opposites in life. No longer is something black OR white, it's black AND white. By recognising and accepting the extremes we are able to enjoy the interplay between them. Life is Yin AND Yang. Both. In a constant interplay.

As we practice Reiki and tread our spiritual path, so we're encouraged to explore the extremes at both ends of many spectra: light-dark, masculine-feminine, material-spiritual, etc.. We begin to see that we need to be aware of and comfortable with both extremes to be able to live our lives naturally. With Reiki we find ourselves going further and further in both directions - doing the mental splits:

* In the spiritual direction we experience a sense of being ever

closer to other creatures, other beings. This 'oneness' becomes not a word or idea but a very real and wonderful experience.

* In the material direction, we're forced to face the *in*humanity within our society - the violence, the denials, the closed nature of so many of our fellow human beings.

Our growing spiritual awareness gives us the inner strength to face the selfishness of much of humanity. Our experiences of 'darkness' around us give us ample opportunity to practice Reiki or otherwise develop our ability to live in light and peace.

This is One World. Our task is to reunite our physical and spiritual selves. When what we're doing assists this process then life IS worth living.

Scrambled

From time to time on the Reiki journey, or indeed on similar paths, our minds will seem, well, scrambled. A mind that's swirling and just not focusing is a sign of major reprogramming work. Such experiences are often associated with the Kundalini experiences too. The Kundalini energy rising, the rebirth of our spiritual selves. Different words, labels and explanations, but the same result. We find energy flowing through us we're not used to. But it *is* natural - it just takes a while to accept and get comfortable with it. Perhaps the best approach to times of mental turmoil is to surrender to them. By not attempting to do anything else, we make the process easier. Try this visualisation to help:

Scrambled Eggs

So, your mind is scrambled. A miss-mash, a mixture of all sorts. Very like scrambled eggs in fact! So picture your brain as a mass of scrambled egg - the two do after all look similar in many respects - a mass of lumps and bumps, with texture and colour variations, but a structure that defies description.

Picture this scrambled egg filling your head. It's well mixed, the 'white' and the yoke no longer separate. The yellow/orange and white now one yellowish hue. The goodness of both parts is in all of the mixture.

Now see the white as our material selves, our physical body. And the yoke as our inner, spiritual, self. For so long separate, as in the egg, they are now one, merged. Our mind, instead of divided into body and soul elements is integrated, re-united with itself.

Feel this mixing happening as your mind swirls. The scrambled egg is being beaten with a fork or a whisk, bringing together our golden centre with our surrounding white, our soul becoming part of our whole being. No longer separate, our Universal essence is now distributed throughout our brain, mind and whole way of thinking and living.

Be with the sensation for as long as you need to be. Before attempting to get up and do anything, open your eyes for a few minutes and re-connect with the world around you. Breath in deeply and release any emotions that may have surfaced. If you feel disoriented, take things easy for a while. You're being reborn - birth of any sort is a traumatic experience! Relish it, enjoy becoming a whole being again.

Mankind's Evolution

This re-alignment process can be seen as part of our evolution - both as individuals and as a species:

Being/Creature	Characterised by
Spiritual Beings	Awareness of all beings Working for the greater good
Intellectuals	Rational brain in control Working for beliefs
Animals	Fight or flight reactions Governed by selfish genes

When we look around at the animal world and human society we see examples of each of these types of being, often to extremes: 'domestic' cats mark their territories, a few aware cats seek out aware humans to be with. Tribal warfare amongst football supporters, legal battles between intellectuals with differing sets of beliefs. World Days of Prayer which transcend all divisions.

What makes Earth so fascinating, and challenging, is that we have the whole spectrum . . . even without human-kind. From base animals to truly evolved spiritual beings. Each individual at their our stage on their path. Awareness means accepting this, being aware that each is where they have to be, learning their lessons their way.

32 - Life-long Learning

In truth, we teach and learn Reiki in all we do. Everybody we meet has something to show us, every relationship of ours is part of our lesson in life. Life-long learning reflects our inner need to continually grow. We become Masters by committing to the process, by allowing our souls to live in us. Any Reiki class is part of this process. So too are formal evening classes, those offered by local authorities. In this chapter we look at bringing Reiki into mainstream education - through adult education.

Adult Education

There is no right and wrong way to teach or learn Reiki. It's more a matter of being aware of the many issues involved. It's also about recognising that the Universe provides us with opportunities to grow and to develop. It *will* stretch us. It will also tempt us: for example to stay stuck in our old ways. Either way we have to tune into our higher self and seek guidance on what's the best thing to do.

It was from this perspective that I faced the opportunity to teach Reiki as Evening Classes. At that time Reiki was predominantly taught as private courses, usually over a weekend. To teach it within a conventional Adult Education situation was new enough, but to spread a 2 or 3 day course over 10 weeks was certainly breaking the rules. I did it because I just *had* to. Many issues came up as I planned and ran the course, each one helping me to see more clearly what was, and wasn't important in teaching Reiki. I share them here to help others broaden their awareness as to what the teaching and learning of healing is all about.

Therapy or what?

A key question is to decide what exactly is being taught. Let's say First Degree Reiki. But for what, as what? At the time these questions were bouncing around my head, the whole issue of standards for Reiki as a therapy was very much in the air. How could Reiki Practitioners be seen to meet the 'standards' expected by the medical profession and by 'the public'. A number of groups were working on 'rules' to 'regulate' our 'industry'. None of it felt right. Besides, practising Reiki as a professional therapist (i.e. charging for treatments) is a very different application to using Reiki for our own self development and/or to help our friends and family. There's the business aspects to consider and ethics and . . . professionalism . . . whatever that meant! It would take more than 10 weeks at one night a week to cover that!

At this time our Local Education Authority were expressing some concern over the running of 'therapy' courses. Not just Reiki (which I was already running as a weekend course for them), but Yoga, Massage, Stress Management, etc. Were we providing a medical service or teaching anything that could be considered a medical practice? If so, we could be in serious trouble. 'Medicine' is outside the scope of Adult Education . . . and quite rightly so. We don't see Evening classes for 'Pharmacy for beginners' or 'Advanced Appendectomy' do we? These are areas requiring extensive training and where professional standards are essential.

These issues seemed to suggest that teaching Reiki in Adult Ed wasn't appropriate and yet I knew Reiki had a place. The weekend courses had gone particularly well and it seemed 'right' to do them. The answer was simple. Not to offer Reiki as a Therapy but as a method for self development. The LEA agreed. 'Therapy' courses are to teach people to help themselves. At about the same time, I'd been made aware of the Buddhist origins to Reiki and thus that Reiki fits very nicely into the idea of personal self and spiritual development. By keeping open to events and possibilities a common ground between Reiki and its roots and the educational establishment had been found. Everybody happy!

Reiki for All

One of the incentives for bringing Reiki into Adult Ed is to make it available to more people. After all, the more folk who are healing themselves the better the quality of life for everyone. Besides, many people find it virtually impossible to 'get away' for a weekend whereas one evening a week is achievable. Offering evening classes brings Reiki to a wider group of individuals . . . *and* it demonstrates that Reiki is not significantly different from any other learning opportunity. Yes, Reiki can change your life . . . but so can learning French, or car maintenance.

The big question was of the financial implications . . . for me as tutor and for the students. By looking at the issues of value and commitment the way forward emerged:

* The cost to students of an evening class were significantly less than those for a private weekend Reiki I course. This is part of the reason why it would allow more to attend. So would they value it? How would they demonstrate their commitment? Once students feel what Reiki can do, they value it. Anyone prepared to come out for 10 weeks running on cold, dark, wet, winter nights demonstrates a commitment.

* Adult Ed tutors are not particularly well paid and running evening classes would bring in far less than teaching the same number privately. But the point is, you wouldn't get them to come privately! The other factor is that Adult Ed has a significant promotional effort and is able to bring Reiki before far more possible students than I ever could. From a financial perspective teaching Reiki I in Adult Ed is a 'loss leader' - it brings in students who may then stay with me to do 2nd Degree and Masters . . . at full rates. OK, a long term investment, but the Universe is always trying to teach me patience.

All these inner debates served merely to satisfy my logical mind that this *was* the right thing to do. The real me knew this anyway.

Elapsed Time

The content of Reiki I as an evening class is not really different to a 2 or 3 day course. About 15 hours actual teaching time. For me. Other tutors might want to expand it to 20 hours (or more) and include some meditation in it, for example, or allow more time for practice and/or debate around the class. Other tutors might want to cut down on some elements. If you're considering attending an evening class and are not sure whether you're going to get the 'full works' ask for a programme. Any decent tutor will welcome the opportunity to discuss your needs and to clarity what they're offering.

The question of time in-between sessions of a class and in particular between attunements is often questioned. Arguments can be put forward to support any particular approach. My own experience is that separating classes works, and works well. This I put down to the fact that evening classes give students much more time to absorb the experience of Reiki and to assimilate it into their lives. Each week they get chance to practice and to come back with questions. Instead of trying to absorb the whole Reiki I Experience in 2 or 3 days they have nearly 3 months in which to reflect on what they're learning. Reiki is like a gourmet meal - it deserves to be savoured.

One argument presented for not stretching a Reiki course over an extended period of time is that 'students will remain open'. The theory sometimes given is that the first attunements 'open up' the student and the last one 'shuts them down'. I have to ask, why shut them down again? The whole point about Reiki is to open us up to our higher selves, to connect us to our inner strength and wisdom. Each attunement does this to an increasing amount. The intent of some Masters in their final attunement however may be to 'close up' or 'close down' their students. If a given student isn't ready, willing or able to consciously work with the Reiki, then maybe a 'closing down' session may be appropriate . . . to reassure the student that all is well. The reality is that the Reiki will do what it has to and each student will respond however they deem fit. We are after all, in Reiki, helping our students to accept responsibility for their own lives and decisions. What is important is to warn students that Reiki *can* change their lives . . . and that the more we fight those changes the more we're likely to suffer.

Follow-up

Having said the above, Reiki Masters do have a responsibility to be aware of their students needs and to provide any follow up advice, etc. that may be necessary. Not to make decisions for their students nor push them unduly to stand on their own feet, but to 'act accordingly'. Again there are no rules. The following ideas apply equally to private or public classes, to evening or weekend courses:

* Regular Sharing Groups - perhaps monthly and preferably locally. An opportunity to meet other Reiki students to compare notes on practice and to give each other treatments.

* Local contacts - provide details of other students who live close by to enable 1 to 1 swaps of treatments.

* Gatherings - to enable sharings between students of different Masters and perhaps other healers. To help show that healing is healing whatever it's called and whoever taught it.

All of these point to a local healing community. When teacher and students live close to each other they are able to work together and with the wider community to everybody's benefit. To live Reiki and grow through Reiki we need to share it. Teaching larger groups from within one community (as usually happens in Evening Classes) does much to foster 'Community Spirit' and bring kindred spirits together. Besides, it's hardly environmentally friendly for both tutor and student to regularly travel huge distances to classes. This is the true application of Reiki. Living the principles in all we do, living simply and naturally: Bringing us all closer to home.

The more the merrier?

What's the ideal size for a Reiki class? Whatever the Universe brings to it. Personally I like to keep class sizes to a manageable number. By which I mean small enough to be able to spend at least some time with each student and make some direct personal contact. This way I can give a 'personal touch' and give them a conscious reassurance that Reiki is for them, individually. My biggest Reiki I class to date has thus been 18. As and when the Universe wants me to handle more, I've no doubt it will provide them.

There are a number of other factors relating to class size:

* Physical Space - Students need to be able to practice giving each other treatments. Even in the school class-rooms used for evening classes this is likely to limit the upper number. 14 to 18 matches what feels comfortable.

* Minimum class size - By their nature, adult Ed classes usually have a minimum enrolment quantity below which they are not viable. This number is large by private class standards, typically 10 to 12. Like it or not, we have to learn to work with such numbers in evening classes.

* Personal views - there is an inevitable trade-off between getting more views in a big class but not being able to share any of them in any depth. Again, this works itself out in the wash: those who need plenty of time to talk will find themselves in a small class. Those who are not yet ready to come out from the safety of a crowd will gravitate to a large class. The Universe has it all in hand, we just have to listen and let it happen.

* Attunements - The thing that worries Reiki teachers most about large classes is doing the attunements. How can they possibly do the full attunement process all those times? The response is to ask "do we need to?". Being faced with the situation is to face our beliefs about what attunements are and what's actually required in an attunement. Reiki is beyond beliefs. Laid down procedures give way to the grace and beauty of Reiki in action when the time comes:

Before my first attunement to my class of 18 I had no clear idea of what I would do. I'd got a piece of music that I usually used for attunements which lasts 45 minutes. Any longer would be a bit much for sitting on hard school-hall (or was it infant sized!) chairs. To do a full, all symbol, initiation for each of the 18 would certainly take too long. And I *knew* it wasn't necessary. In the event I just put on the music and let the Reiki guide me. Yes, I connected with each student by walking around behind them and placing hands on each of their heads in turn. Yes, the symbols were used at some stage within the whole process. But what took the place of the 'normal' process was a wonderful shared experience. Each of the 4 attunements, over the 10 weeks, was different, in some way embracing all the features of the 4 'normal' attunements. But to define this logically would be to miss the point. An attunement is when the initiating Master connects his students and himself to The Oneness. With that intent and an open mind, that is what happens. Does it matter exactly how? The feedback from the students highlighted that it does not. The power and beauty of their experiences every bit as varied and rewarding as attunement experiences done 'the proper way'. So much for rules.

Evening Class Masters?

At Reiki II and Masters I tend to teach much smaller numbers, which are not (yet) possible through Adult Education. It seems more appropriate when we are talking about Reiki in our lives that each student has an opportunity to discuss, in some depth, what Reiki means for them. This is very difficult with large classes. Of course, it could be argued that Reiki works beyond the level of intellectual debate and thus that such discussions are unnecessary to a good Reiki class. You pays your money and you takes your choice . . . often literally.

Reiki for Children

The logical progression from Reiki in Adult Education is Reiki in all schools. What a wonderful idea to have all children encouraged to heal themselves and tune into their inner self as part of their main education. Instead of being taught to suppress our intuition and uniqueness they could be enabled to grow naturally from the start. 'Right First Time' as Total Quality Management would put it! So much of the effort most of us expend on our spiritual path is about undoing unbalanced thought processes, about letting go of notions of control and material supremacy. To learn, from a babe, that we are spiritual beings and that the life energy (Reiki, God, whatever we want to call it) is within and around all of us . . . doesn't that sound like a really useful thing to do?

And it's beginning to happen! In the UK, the National Curriculum has a requirement for Social, Moral and Spiritual education. Already most schools include lessons on the range of religions now found in most towns. Many head teachers are also introducing relaxation techniques into their study programme. Meditation in schools is no longer a dream. Any technique that helps a child to calm down is very welcome to hard pushed teachers.

Many Reiki Masters offer attunements for children. For younger children in particular, full training isn't necessary - they don't need all the intellectual stuff that goes with it. Not because they're not able to understand it (many young children are) but because they're still naturally open to Reiki and receptive to what it means - they haven't got wrong impressions to be overcome. The feedback I get is that many children, particularly of Reiki trained parents, *ask* for Reiki training themselves and take to it as a duck to water. Which isn't at all surprising.

Reiki - Without Rules

33 - One Society

One of the many challenges in becoming a Reiki Master is in accepting that the wholeness that is human life embraces all aspects of society. We are *all* one, including multi-national companies, drugs barons, beggars, etc. The aim is to be able to look anyone and everyone in the eye, to accept them and to respect them. Now that's a job for Reiki! As we learn, see how we are all interconnected, then the harsh reality of divisions, and denials that are society can be hard to tolerate. Gradually however, bit by bit, we can take on board the fact that everybody is doing what they have to do in their own way.

In this chapter we look at how Reiki ties in with the wider aspects of society:

Integrated Health Care

Having spent most of this book saying that 'There are No Rules', I'd now like to talk about standards!

Before taking up Reiki, I was in the Quality Assurance profession. I spent much of my time working with and on standards. I sat on and even chaired national and European standards groups . . . I know where they go wrong. . . . and where they *can* be of benefit.

It is in helping to bring Reiki and other forms of healing into Health Care generally that standards may well have an important role to play. Through the implementation of their own Occupational Standards other therapies are becoming accepted by the conventional medical profession: Reflexology, Aromatherapy, Hypnotherapy and Homeopathy for example. Increasingly these therapies are being offered alongside the drugs and surgical treatments in our health clinics and hospitals.

There is another trend that is encouraging and in keeping with the growing interest in Reiki: Health Self Management. The concept is simple and certainly supported by holistic therapists: there is much that patients with chronic conditions can do for themselves. Through looking at and improving our lifestyle (diet, exercise, creative activities, etc) and attitudes, we can encourage our own healing abilities. When our health is seen as part of our whole being and we treat it as such, we *can* improve our Quality of Life.

Initially with Arthritis care and then with other chronic conditions, Health Self Management has successfully demonstrated that when encouraged to work on their own well-being patients can become more confident and happy in their lives. Although still a comparatively new approach, an increasing number of self-help and support groups for a range of conditions are beginning to try and promote this path.

The role of standards in this development is not just to reassure the established health services, but also to act as forum for exchange of ideas. The standardisation process helps all 'sides' to see and appreciate the views and experiences of others. In the UK the Reiki Federation is to be congratulated on their enlightened (i.e. realistic!) approach to the subject.

Care in the Community

Reiki encourages us to take charge of our own health and well-being. It also enables each of us to take a more active role in the healing of our loved ones. Many take Reiki classes so that they can give treatments to their friends and family and thus reduce their dependence on the health service. Surely this is the ultimate 'Care in the Community' - each family and/or neighbourhood with its own trained healer who can help those feeling under the weather. Such a scenario has many advantages:

* Many conditions will be treatable without having to travel to surgeries or health centres - something which can be difficult for many in some remote communities.

* Reiki healing energy is free. It's use could cut drugs bills (and their side effects) significantly. The cost of Reiki training would be quickly

repaid.

* Reiki is an holistic approach, so looks at the emotional and environmental causes of a condition. If the healer lives in the same community then they will be more aware of relevant factors and thus be in a better position to encourage more appropriate 'treatment' - in terms of changes to life-style, relationship issues, etc.

* The more members of a community who practise Reiki, the more harmonious that community will tend to be. i.e. it's a great preventative approach to community health care.

Thus a community takes responsibility for its own health. Our well-being is in our own hands.

There ARE Rules!

Of course, there has to be an exception to the rule that there are no rules. We know only too well that much of society is governed by and places much faith in its laws and rules. Where and when individuals are not willing or able to discipline themselves, then imposed discipline, unfortunately, seems necessary . . . or at least is deemed necessary by those conditioned to rules. But let's look at the bigger picture with two examples:

I was watching a programme about vice - how the UK police coped with street prostitutes. They'd catch them soliciting, bring them in and charge them. A few hours later the girls would be back out on the game . . . earning money to pay their fine. A clear example of where punishing individuals for not following rules actually serves to make the situation worse.

This is the old, established way of tacking an issue. Something makes us uneasy, doesn't meet with our idea of what's right so we slap on some form of restriction. We impose rules, we introduce some form of protection mechanism. It doesn't work. It's akin to the allopathic approach to medicine - treating the symptom doesn't get rid of the problem. Hiding a problem from view merely prolongs the agony.

The aware approach to any situation that presents itself as discord, be it in society or our bodies, is to face it. Seek out and identify the true cause of the disharmony and find a way of restoring the harmony.

Mankind's 'divide and conquer' approach has gone far enough. It's now time to 'work together and solve'. The same applies in matters of health, crime or business. The approach is much needed in the banking sector for example:

In 1998 UK banks introduced a rule which said that their high street branches would only a accept cheques being paid in if either the cheque or the account was with them. Previously, and very sensibly, you could pay any cheque into any bank, with maybe a small charge if it wasn't your own bank. Money's money isn't it? Apparently not! Banks only seem interested if, in some way, it's *their* money! When I was told this I looked in disbelief at the bank staff. But, never mind convenience for the customer, rules are rules. All they would say by way of explanation is that it was "for security". It's as if one bank couldn't trust another with *their* money! OK, so maybe they had a fraud problem which was worrying them. The old human instincts obviously kicked into place. Fear! A problem! Oh, lets introduce a rule to deal with it. Lets tighten up our procedures. Have they never tried holding sand in the hand . . . the tighter you clench your fist the less sand you actually keep.

Look around at any aspect of human life. Where you see rigid control, hard & fast rules, divisions between those involved, there too you see higher levels of stress, dissatisfied customers . . . and huge amounts of wasted time and often futile effort trying to maintain the rule. Enough is enough. Yes, we need guidelines. Yes every member of our society needs to act responsibly. But it is human nature to only respect rules and those who make them if, in return, those institutions respect us.

So respect and a real understanding of any 'problem' is the spiritual approach. A quest for truth. I'm not suggesting that this is easy. It can be a long, hard, job to get to the root cause of illness, societal unrest or a specific crime. But not to do so allows this disharmony to

Reiki - Without Rules

continue. Rules that guide and help us to work together, to understand each other are useful tools to a more enlightened society. Rules used as an excuse for not facing reality are part of the cause of the problem.

The reality, however, is that rules of one form or another still impact on our lives - daily. What's the enlightened approach to them?

* Enlighten those involved! Sometimes it's appropriate to challenge the rule and help those promoting it to see the bigger picture. When done in a calm, positive, manner, often we *can* make a difference. Find a way forward that makes life easier for those who have to work with the rule. e.g. get involved in the standards making process, offer your services as a Consumer representative, etc.

* Nothing. i.e. just accept the situation. The true 'Jobsworth' character will not be impressed by any amount of reasoning or appealing.

"*Just* accept." If only it were that easy! Rules are thrown at us by the Universe to test us, to try our patience. To 'pass' this test we need to respond with unconditional love. Often hard work, particularly when faced with bureaucratic red-tape and inflexibility. This is the way of those in such lines of work. All we can do is to put ourselves in their shoes, to try to understand why the rule is the way it is. There is always a reason, even if the logic behind it is limited or distorted. Through understanding we gain acceptance. Through love, with the help of Reiki treatments, we tolerate . . . even the most frustrating of officials.

Unconditional Love

Wouldn't it be wonderful to live in a world of unconditional love. To be part of a society where there are no lies, no selfishness, no aggression. Where there is no anger, no deceit, no worry. It is possible. Such would be, will be, an enlightened world. With so many individuals now on a spiritual path (be it Reiki or whatever), so more and more people are committed to living to love, loving to live . . . and learning whatever lessons that path takes us through.

Reiki - Without Rules

Unconditional Love - loving whoever, whenever, however the here and now requires, is again taking full responsibility for our lives . . . and for our part of how society operates. This is the awareness approach to improving our quality of life. Say we want to reduce our level of fear and worry. The old approach, linking responsibility with blame and societal structure, would have said: more bobbies on the beat, tighten security, lock up those responsible for the crime. i.e. the cause of fear is seen as the criminal. Is it? The cause of fear is a lack of confidence in the person experiencing the fear. An enlightened person has no fear. Putting up fences and installing more alarms does not solve the problem. Taking up self defence, going to classes on assertiveness, Reiki, etc will - slowly but surely - help to face and rise above the fear.

And the criminals? Respond to them with unconditional love! By showing them respect, by understanding that their behaviour reflects their own state of mind. By helping them to feel wanted members of a community, by encouraging them to express their energies positively, *for* the community, their need to offend will (slowly but surely) diminish. Around the world, many examples of 'community service' and bringing offenders to 'make good' with their victims is proving very successful. Open, honest, loving. Recognising that we are all interconnected. Truly enlightened folks do not tend to commit offences against society.

No Secrets

Secrecy, and the perceived need for it, comes from human egos. It is part of the competitive nature of humans. It belongs only to those individuals and groups who seek to control, to 'beat' others. Secrecy has no significant place in a soul centred society. How can it? As we all become enlightened, so we all become highly intuitive. As we connect to our higher selves, so our telepathic abilities develop . . . to the extent that we *know* what others are thinking and feelings - at least, as and when we need to. The emerging spiritual reality is one based on honesty and openness. Sharing freely for the greater good. I would like to share two examples:

I run occasional gatherings of local Reiki Masters - as an

opportunity to meet, to share our experiences and ideas. Although there are no rules at such events, the underlying theme is of freedom. As one Master put it "It's great to be able to say what I really think". Isn't it! And why shouldn't we? All those doubts we have that our 'non-standard' way of doing things is 'right' soon evaporate as we find that others not only question perceived wisdom but have also had experiences that 'prove' that the only 'right way' is whatever is right for us at any given moment . . . whether we are talking about how we do Reiki treatments, attunements . . . or whatever.

It's not just in the rarefied world of Reiki Masters that openness is seen as the way forward. The second example concerned a meeting in Northampton's ancient Guildhall - to discuss the town's response to the (then) new National Lottery funds for 'Healthy Living Centres'. Over a hundred folks from all branches of health and social care listened and shared their thoughts on what healthy living was about and how we could tackle inequalities. The conclusion? We need to work together, to share openly. To improve our quality of life (all of us) we need to break down the barriers between different official bodies, different disciplines, different cultures, etc. We are *all* human beings seeking to love and be loved.

We are all different and need those differences respected, but unity comes from celebrating our diversity, through partnership. Secrecy prevents a free flow of energy - be it unconditional love or information. Mankind's progression to an enlightened society thus require that we share information freely between us . . . only then can we see the full story. We cannot become whole beings until we examine the whole picture: Health workers talking to social worker; teachers working alongside doctors; environmentalist sharing aims and practices with businessman. This is the trend as we enter the 3rd Millennium. This is the way forward. One World which we can all help to create by building bridges and knocking down barriers . . . in how *we* live *Our* lives.

Reiki - Without Rules

Un-secret Service

But what does this mean in practice? *Saying what we mean and meaning what we say.* Yes, sometimes it might be appropriate to 'keep mum', even to tell a white lie . . . if that is what our inner voice is telling us to do. Being open and honest is about doing what we *have* to do, saying what we *have* to say. Without fear or favour. Being afraid of hurting somebody's feelings is still a fear. If something we say is hurtful to another person, that's their issue. If we feel guilty about it, then it's ours. If we can't say what we really feel to a friend, then are they a true friend? . . . or rather are *we* being a true friend? OK, being brutally honest may loose us some so-called friends. But loving somebody isn't about being lovey dovey all the time. Sometimes we have to be cruel to be kind. Tell a few home truths. Bring the truth out into the open.

Seeing The Truth

Whilst writing this book I kept coming across the idea that we can tell whether somebody is telling the truth by looking at where their eyes are pointing. If they rise to the left, then they're delving into genuine memory, if up to the right, then the thought is an imaginary one. As with other theories on the left/right split within the brain, there is probably some truth in this. There is little doubt that for most of us our rational/logical mind is over-developed whereas the intuitive/creative mind is poorly developed. Worse than that, the two parts often don't talk to each other!

Thus any technique that develops our right brain and/or helps the various parts of our brain to work as one are likely to help us become 'One', whole. But how does this idea help us to use all our minds fully?

Take a situation where we're unsure of what action to take. Maybe we're sensing, in our mind, a direction. Perhaps an image of some-one. Should we contact that person now or not? So, *where* in our mind is that image? On the left side or the ride side? Which side isn't really important, but unless the image *fills* the mind, then we have a clear indication that the idea is lop-sided, not representative of the truth. If, on the other hand(!) we have an inner knowing about something and that idea can be 'seen', 'heard' or 'felt' in both sides of our mind, then it's far more likely that we're 'picking up' the truth. Here we have a thought worth acting on!

Of One Mind

Say we have a thought that won't go away. How do we decide whether and how to act on it?

Shut your eyes and breath deeply. Breath in truth, breath out mist, doubts, etc. Place one hand on either side of the head in whatever position is comfortable. Feeling the energy flow in the hands and in the head. Notice where and how the energy flows, listen to any ringing (tinnitus) and see how this changes or moves about.

Now return to the original thought. Is it still there? If not, it wasn't of any significance! If it is, focus on it, locate the thought in the head - left or right? front or back? Visualise the Reiki healing energy (from the hands if that helps) focusing on that point and then spreading. Try to move the thought IN your mind. Perhaps you can see it as a purple or yellow spot - imagine this spot moving until it is between the eyes. Centre the colour, balance the thought. Now listen to it. Is it the same thought you started with? The more off-centred it was to begin with, the more likely that it's changed significantly.

Focus again on your breathing, taking the attention away from the brain and bring it back into your body. Take your hands from your head and rest, allowing the process to complete without conscious interruption. If the mind wonders, think 'peace' and allow calmness to spread through you - mind AND body. Take time. Allow your mind to make peace with itself.

Mystical Magic

Much of the call for secrecy surrounding Reiki and other such practices revolves around the idea that it's a magical, mystical, a thing only accessible to the chosen few. This may have been the case in medieval times. It is not true now. As we pass the year 2000 so the whole of human-kind is getting ready to live the magic and mystery of our spiritual nature. Now we have One World emerging. It is no longer 'weird' or 'strange' to have or use psychic powers. Our healing, telepathic and other abilities are becoming accepted as a part of us. Yes they are magical. Yes they are special, often sacred, certainly gifts to be respected and treated with care. But they are no longer secret. Reiki, God's essence, is in each of us. That isn't something to keep secret, that's a fact to sing and shout about.

Remembrance

In the UK on 11th November 1998 it is estimated that three quarters of the population observed two minutes silence at 11 O'clock. In shops, streets, schools; at banks, railway stations and in homes across the country people of all ages and backgrounds stopped what they were doing to remember those who had died 80 years before in the Great War . . . and in the many armed conflicts since.

Perhaps 'remember' is the wrong word, since vast numbers, thankfully, had and have no personal recollection of what life in war-time is like. And yet they chose to reflect for those 2 minutes. The conclusion has to be that we, as a nation, needed to focus our attention on the horrors of war . . . that we might commit ourselves to peace. It is a sign of the general rise in consciousness of the human species. Finally we are realising that war solves nothing. Now, with the new millennium, we can see an alternative. Within us all is the love possible to bring about a world at peace with itself. That 2 minutes public expression of hope mirrors the many hours each week that many now devote to improving themselves and/or to working for peace and harmony in their lives and the world around.

Being reminded of how so many gave their lives that we might be free helps put our own lives into perspective. It helps us to ask what freedom is, what life is. More than at any other time in our history mankind is aware of the choices he faces. Gradually the truth is dawning that freedom often means making sacrifices.

Although armed conflicts still affect the world, fighting now is more likely in market place and court-rooms. The battles are increasingly mental and emotional rather than physical . . . but none the less painful for that. Shell shock has been largely replaced by work induced stress as a cause of mental breakdown . . . but challenges remain. That's life. Remembrance of the 11th of the 11th 1918 brings the harsh realities of life to the fore. Sometimes we just do what we have to do . . . for King and Country . . . or for Our Father in Heaven. On days like this the man in the street starts asking "what's it all for?" and in doing so moves one step closer to his maker . . . for only God has the answer.

Anti-Establishment?

Some readers may feel that in discouraging the following of rules that I'm anti-establishment. It depends what you mean by 'The Establishment'. If you mean those who are in business and government for their own ends, who 'use' others with no regard for their needs, then I'm anti establishment. If you mean the Jobsworth type who insist that you do things the way they've always been done even thought such ways are no longer relevant, then yes, I'm anti-establishment.

If, however, you mean organisations that encourage communications between those of different views, that enable each individual to reach their potential then I'm *pro* establishment. There is good in all things . . . and a reason for everything. Even those aspects of 'the establishment' which constrain, restrict and limit us have their purpose . . . and until we're able to accept responsibility for our actions, we have to accept the rule of law through society.

Often when we start on our spiritual journey we draw a distinction between those committed to living spiritually and the rest - the conventional world. However, there is no such distinction. We all ARE . . . Different. Some so called 'spiritual' folk leave much to be desired. Some 'conventional' folk have a genuine loving nature.

34 - Manifest Joy

Many other self development books talk of bringing your dreams into reality, about our lives being manifestations of our thoughts. There is both much truth and considerable dangers to such an approach. In Reiki we certainly find, as we come aware of our thoughts, how much our life results from how we think. It is thus not unreasonable to assume that positive thoughts will result in a positive life! But what do we mean by 'positive thought'? And who are we to decide what is a 'positive life' and what isn't?

Many 'roads to happiness' teach us to decide what we want and go for it. To make affirmations, to rise above fears, to have faith in ourselves. All of these are worthwhile as intents along our path in life.

Affirmations are akin to the Reiki Principles, these can be very helpful in stopping the mind focusing on 'failures'. For example, if we are experiencing a cash flow difficulty to affirm that 'there is abundance in my life' can help to counter the fears associated with having no money. But to deny genuine financial difficulties will achieve nothing. Before we use affirmations we need to be sure that we *have* faced any fears or anger. We need to be sure that the topic of our affirmation is realistic. Affirmations are no substitute for lack of awareness of the real issues in our life. Thus, if we are short of cash and actually *need* to take action to improve the situation, no amount of affirmations will resolve our money shortage. Positive thinking is no alternative to doing things we actually *need* to do.

However, given that we are in tune with our true needs, given that we have faced our fears and other feelings, *then* we *can* manifest all manner of things into our life. The Universe provides everything we need for our life's journey. When we let go of unrealistic expectations, when we let go of the dreams we've been conditioned into, we become open to all that God can provide: joy, peace, abundance of companionship, wealth, health and happiness.

By focusing on these qualities, without any preconceived idea as to the form they will take, we allow the Universe to satisfy our needs in ways that will most benefit us.

What if, on the other hand, we have this dream of an 'ideal' partner, an 'ideal' house, and 'ideal' job and go all out to get it. Sure, enough, if we put all our will and energies into the project we might find that the Universe gives us what we want. We then find, more often than not, that what we thought would be 'ideal' is nothing of the sort. Our ideas on what would be 'perfect' for us are nearly always based on limited thoughts, on dreams, on unrealistic expectations. We tend in such dreams only to see that which we want to see . . . and not the other aspects of the situations. Thus we might get our £100,000 a year job . . . but find it left us with no time to the family. Or we might meet and marry our model partner to find they were hopeless with money and boring in bed.

But, some of you might say, isn't it our dreams that inspire us to take risks and move on in life? Absolutely. Our 'dreams', our 'visions' are important motivators on our journey through life. The danger is in seeing them as plans, as fixed objectives. We need to assess our dreams both in the harsh light of reality and in the wondrous light of wisdom. We need to compare these dreams with what's actually possible, here and now. This is where Reiki comes into it's own. For Reiki connects us fully to reality, it shows us the truth. Instead of allowing one-sided dreams to take us over it helps us to become aware of all aspects of a situation. From this place of calm we *know* what we need to do *now*. And that's often all we can know for certain. The future will take care of itself.

The self development programmes that are most effective are those that encourage us to 'live for the now' or better, live *in* the now. The distinction is important. Those who live *for* the present tend to take what they can get and sod the consequences. This is *not* what living in the here and now is about. When we focus on the moment we are in, in Reiki, we become aware of *all* aspects of that moment - including all relevant past events and all relevant possible futures. By doing what we *have* to at each moment, we automatically take into account everybody else who might be involved.

We manifest joy in our lives by focusing our love into each moment. By following life and loving each moment of it . . . in whatever way is appropriate, we will find ourselves fulfilled. This is unconditional love. Happiness as a state of mind. The Buddhist detachment from outcome. The truth is that *nothing really matters.* Only when we accept that will we truly manifest joy in our lives.

The Experience

To adapt to the above way of life means to surrender control of our lives to the Universe. This can be scary. It can also cause our egos to fight for grim life. In 20th Century society we were conditioned to be in control. Man over nature, intelligence over intuition. But it doesn't work, does it? Man may have an incredible brain, we may be able to do all sorts of wonderful things . . . but that doesn't make us God.

But God is in us. We are part of The One. Our needs are met by The Universe. So why bust a gut trying to work things out ourselves? To surrender to the Universe is be to free.

I could not have said this 10 years ago. I would not have said it before getting seriously into Reiki. It is only after 3 years of fairly continuous Reiki (both self treatments and giving attunements) that enabled me to let go, to admit that 'I', meaning my logical, independent, self, doesn't know anything. Through the Reiki Experience I have learnt that the universe *does* provide for me. I have learn that the freedom that we strive for is not a physical thing but a state of mind: having a mind clear of 'shoulds' and 'oughts'. Being able to just 'go with the flow' and enjoy it. It has required much hard work in letting go of things and ideas I used to think were important, but all this fades into insignificance when we can live in light, as light. When we live with a sparkle in out eyes, eyes smile back. When we are able to respond naturally to events around us we are warmly welcomed and loved in return. Reiki is about truly living; being at peace with ourselves and with the world.

Reiki - Without Rules

Sensations

The experience of being is at all levels - with those around us, with the world at large . . . and, perhaps most importantly with and within ourselves. One of the most common descriptions used by new comers to Reiki to describe their treatment is 'a sense of well-being'. They, and anybody who uses Reiki regularly, feel 'safe' . . . for we are protected by the Universe.

As was discussed in Chapter 12 (The Aspects of Reiki), the aim is to feel this sense of security all the time. Wherever we are, whatever we're doing. For our life on earth to feel that we're in heaven. So that our home is where the heart is . . . which is everywhere.

In life we seek to be reunited with out maker, to come home. To feel at One. This is possible through Reiki.

Some of the experiences are scary to those new to Reiki just because they are new and different. Many of us fear to surrender to anything or anybody . . . in which case it is an issue they have to face. The most happy people I know are those who have surrendered.

Enhancement

Reiki enhances whatever we do. i.e. it tunes us into the spirit of whatever activity we're engaged in and helps us to become part of it. This is particularly true of Complementary Therapy. Thus, with the experience of Reiki, Hypnotherapists become more aware of their clients' relevant emotions and memories and Masseurs are more able to tune into the physical needs of each client, for example. Many therapists of many different disciplines take up Reiki - not to add to their list of therapeutic services but to enhance their existing abilities . . . and to develop themselves as whole people . . . which will also improve their effectiveness as therapists and healers.

This enhancing quality helps to bring out the deeper significance of other therapies, both during treatments and as a therapist develops their skills. By focusing on Hypnotherapy or Yoga, the practitioner is able to really explore that subject, get to the heart of it. Reiki facilitates the learning experience and opens up any student to the holistic nature of whatever is being studied. *ANY* therapy or spiritual practice can be a path to enlightenment. Where some other therapy has been chosen as a specialist subject, Reiki is an ideal catalyst for change and personal growth as part of the overall process. Choose what feels right for you and explore it, inside and out . . . Reiki will always support this process. If it doesn't, then it could be that this learning process isn't the right one for you . . . or you've not found the right Reiki teacher.

Likewise authors become more channels to divine words, artists find their works flow more easily. Reiki is an enhancer. It brings out the best in us . . . the genius within us all. It's just a matter of finding out what it is we are a genius in or of.

Reiki & Relationships

When I was offered the chance to take Reiki II, I was taken by the claim that it could help with addictions. I knew I had a problem that needed all the help I could get: I was addicted to a pretty face. I used to fall in love with any charming lady who took any sort of interest in me.

Three years later, I was able to admit to preferring the company of women but without forming any attachment. Through Reiki I've been able to face the reality of each attraction, learn the appropriate lesson, then move on . . . whilst remaining good friends with the lady concerned. Gradually my idealised image of a 'perfect woman' or my dream partner has been challenged. Now I see that 'perfection' (if it exists at all) is the here and now . . . and whoever, or whatever, the Universe has provided.

Reiki helps us to appreciate all 'Aspects of Love' and thus to put romantic/erotic love into perspective.

Nobody's Fault

As we tread the Reiki road, or any other path of awareness we see how we are only responsible for what we say, think and do. Not for what effect they may have on others. The other way of looking at this is: we cannot blame anybody (else) for how we feel.

At the same time, Reiki often helps us to see the truth about situations. We begin to see for example that how we behave is as a result of our conditioning . . . we either do things because that's how things were always done by our parents (for example) or do the opposite . . . for the same reason! But to acknowledge *why* we behave a certain way is a major step towards growing out of unrealistic behaviour. Blaming those involved is not part of the process. It achieves nothing, or less than nothing.

Similarly there's no point blaming ourselves. We all do our best. Everything just *is.*

Many people would be shocked by such an attitude, thinking that by saying such things I'm condoning all manner of illegal and/or immoral acts. I am not. I'm just suggesting that, if we look hard enough, there is a reason for everything . . . and for everybody's behaviour. The holistic approach to any condition - be it physical or emotional (including so called 'anti-social behaviour') is to look for the root cause of that behaviour. Not just in upbringing and social environment, but in our soul journey. What are we, as individual spiritual beings, here to learn? When this question is asked, so many health and behavioural difficulties can be seen in a much clearer light. Reiki helps us to peel away the layers of self deception and of denial and see the reality of the situation. From a place of truth we stand a far better chance of moving on, of learning our lessons.

Better than drink!

So, where does my addiction to pretty faces fit in? Considering the grief I caused various ladies along the way, by my often pathetic and clinging ways, it was certainly an anti-social behaviour. Facing it has forced me to acknowledge my spiritual self. It has enabled me to put romantic love into perspective. By seeing the love that is in all things, having a conventional romantic relationship is less important. When, in Reiki, you are able to reach that place of bliss, what need of unrequited romance, or drink or drugs? We fall into these addictions in an attempt to find a better reality, a place of security and happiness. Such a place does exist and exists without the need to take any substance.

In "Perceptions" Aldous Huxley describes the effects of the drug mescaline. The state induced is one of wonderful colours, of euphoria. It makes the world seem a wonderful place. This altered state of consciousness is not that different from the sense of One-ness that comes through Reiki. In Reiki we have the potential to provide drug takers with what they seek . . . in a safe way.

But IS Reiki safe? IS Reiki itself addictive? Many who have taken to Reiki will admit that it has become part of their life. They would say that even if they wanted to, they couldn't be without it. Because being with Reiki is being your true self. To *not* 'have Reiki' would be to live in a state of unreality. The Reiki world is the real world. What makes it acceptable is that the world everybody else sees remains there too.

Reiki and Play

Hopefully, through this book, you've seen that Reiki isn't so much a subject to be learnt but a way of life to be remembered . . . and lived. At times it may mean hard work, at times it will bring a peace and calm deeper than many of us have previously imagined. Another important facet of our lives that Reiki will help to bring out is our sense of fun.

As we 'loosen up' and rise above our constraining conditioning, so our inner child comes back into our lives. Life *should* be fun! Reiki helps us to enjoy ourselves whether at work, rest or play. Quite likely we'll have some old ideas about play and games which are doing us no favours; but as we play in the spirit of Reiki we'll find the true sense of play which is beneath all real games. It differs from what is often considered a 'game' or 'play':

* True play is spontaneous, is creative, is expressive. There may be rules to the game, but they're more likely to be ones that encourage us to break conventional rules. e.g. in Blind Man's Buff you have to

go around blind-folded and use your hands to find people. Touch is required where it's usually frowned upon. Play helps us to explore our senses.

* It's not the winning that matters. Whilst competitive sport can help to bring out the best in people and is thus important for character building, it can often take away the fun aspect of sports and games. In fact, if you enjoy what you're doing you're more likely to be relaxed and in tune with your inner resources . . . and thus to win! However, a 'good' game is one that is enjoyable for all - no matter who wins.

* Simplicity. Games do not have to use boards, balls or any gadgets. When we use our imaginations we don't need props. 'New Games', for example (see Contacts Section), is a series of games for all ages that uses little, if any, equipment . . . and yet they encourage co-operation, team building, trust building and much more. Through playing 'New Games' my inner child has really come alive again and an hidden ability is 'coming out' - to have fun in *all* I do. Well, that's where it's heading: unfortunately it still has rather a lot of "shut up and be quiet" conditioning to undo!

* Child-*like* not Child-*ish*. We're talking about the innocence of children, about a natural sense of adventure. Child-like play flows and hurts no-one. Our inner child is part of our inner/higher self that will protect us, it will also connect us with people and places around us. It is inclusive. Child-ish play, by contrast, is when the ego takes over, when the game is played for that person's self gratification. It is often exclusive, with pleasure taken at the expense of others - this is not natural play.

Our playful spirit is a close relative to the unconditional love that comes when we live with heart and soul. Everybody can benefit from play. If they're not doing so, you might want to look at the methods and motivations of the game under way. A suitable intent for play is that everybody involved (including spectators and neighbours for example) come away feeling uplifted. Again, for the greater good. Reiki helps us to focus on this goal, whether the prize at stake is a world championship . . . or a can of pop.

Reiki - Without Rules

There is no conflict between play and Reiki. On the contrary, they are mutually supportive, each helping us to be true to the different aspects of ourselves - at appropriate moments. It *may* be appropriate, for example, to use play within a Reiki course to connect to our playful spirit - or to do some Reiki healing during a game to help rise above fears of loosing.

If Reiki isn't helping you have fun in your life, there's something wrong somewhere.

So how would you use Reiki to access the playful spirit:

Bringing Out the Inner Child

This exercise can be used as a personal visualisation or as a group visualisation. It could also be used as the basis for group play - i.e. bringing the sense of play out of the imagination into reality.

Get comfortable and close your eyes. Breathe slowly and deeply. Allow your hands to fall naturally and give yourself a Reiki healing in that position. Imagine yourself surrounded by a playful energy. (Use the Reiki Symbols if it helps). You have with you the Angel of Play. She says "You could be anywhere in the Universe. Where are you?". Let an image or sense of somewhere come to mind - it could a moon-base, a desert camp; Atlantis, or anywhere. Focus on the place and develop the picture. Add in sounds, scents, movements.

The Angel of Play speaks again "Within your play world, Who are You? You could be anyone - a street urchin, a king, Superwoman, an angel like me!" Get a sense of whether you're young, old . . . or ageless. You are not just playing the part of this person (or being) you ARE this being.

Allow the scene to move on. You're interacting with those around you, laughing, dancing, enjoying yourself. How? Are you the star of the world's juggling convention or a king playing marbles with his grandchildren. Anything. Whatever comes to mind. Play. Enjoy.

Allow your inner child full reign. There are no restrictions, no rules, in this fantasy world. You are free to enjoy life.

After a suitable 'play-time', see yourself saying goodbye to those you've been playing with. Smile in farewell knowing that you can go back to join them at any time. Open your eyes and reconnect to the world around you now.

To use this for group play, ask for suggestions from the group as to where you are and agree this between you. Then each decide who you are within this place. You can then either

a) tell each other your identities and then act out a scene involving them all   or

b) keep your identity secret. Each member of the group would then take it in turn to *become* that part, to mime it, for the rest of the group to guess the role.

35 - Awareness

Reiki can certainly be considered as a path to awareness, but what does that mean? What exactly are we becoming more aware of?

* Who and what we are. Our true inner/higher self. Our soul and its needs.

* Our mind and body. The physical and emotional reflections of our soul and its needs. We become aware, for example, not just that we are getting nervous but why we are having such feelings. We become more able to distinguish between genuine sensations of the moment and conditioned reactions. As we become more aware so a higher level of consciousness opens up in us - one which monitors our own thoughts and feelings and helps us to see the truth.

* The world around us - all aspects of it. We become aware that our chosen life-style and path is but one of millions. We begin to see that each and every being is on their own life journey, doing *their* best to do what *they* have to. We become aware not just of the differences between other people and ourselves but aware of their needs. As we become aware of their soul purpose so we are more able to accept them as they are and live in harmony with a greater part of humanity.

* The natural world. The changing seasons, the power and unpredictability of the forces of nature. It is no coincidence that British TV has had more programmes on natural phenomena - tornadoes, volcanoes, earthquakes, etc. in recent years. We are becoming aware that these forces *are* greater than those of man . . . and that what man does can influence our natural environment. The 'Green Movement' is a very real example of our growing awareness of our place in the natural world.

* Other dimensions. We are becoming more consciously aware and accepting of our psychic abilities. We are happy to believe in UFOs and aliens, in ESP and reincarnation. We find ourselves having Out

Of Body Experiences and will even share our experiences of Astral Travel. We are becoming aware that there is more to life than the three dimensions of earthly existence and of the linear time used by humans. Many would still argue that angels, aliens and so on are all in the mind . . . maybe they are . . . *it doesn't matter where they are!* The point is we have become aware of other levels of consciousness. We now know that our minds can access other worlds, other dimensions. We are aware that the Universe is multidimensional, that we are not the only intelligent life forms. In fact we may be a rather insignificant form of life compared to others. We are becoming aware of our true place in life.

* Of God. As we become aware of all these other aspects of life, so we also recognise that they are all part of a greater picture and are all interconnected. We begin to see beneath the ritual of religions to the underlying truth of spirituality.

All this growth in awareness is happening all around us all the time. Life itself is a path to greater awareness. Every challenge we face, every opportunity to grow provides learning experiences from which our awareness develops. By being aware that this is what life is about, we see our lives in a new, broader, perspective. We can see that new relationships, recurring dreams, 'accidents', in *everything* that happens to us, is an opportunity us to see the bigger picture and to grow up. For 'growing up' is about becoming more aware.

But if it's happening anyway, why do we need Reiki, or other therapies and tools like it? *To help us become aware that it's happening!* Although many are now making major efforts to 'sort themselves out' or to 'get healthy', often this process is still seen in physical terms. By seeing it as part of our soul's progress we immediately take a major step on the awareness path. Reiki helps us to see ourselves as spiritual beings growing in awareness . . . rather than as physical humans doing human things.

But do we *need* to be consciously aware of all of this? *Probably not.* Many are growing in the way and at the pace they need to without any intellectual debate on consciousness and awareness. There are many lovely people who just *are*. We all, I hope, know some: always ready with a kindly and genuine smile, always honest and open, firm but kind; Probably working with nature in some way (gardener, craftsman, etc.). Such individuals are so aware (although perhaps not consciously) of who and what they are that they don't *need* to philosophise or 'sort themselves out'.

So Reiki is for those who know there's something wrong in their life, who sense that they are not in tune with who and what they are meant to be. Reiki, particularly as a self treatment and self development tool, shines light onto our situation and opens us up to higher levels of awareness.

But are other philosophies and therapies as useful? *They may be, for you, now.* There are no right and wrong paths, only whatever is appropriate for you at a given moment. If in doubt, then reflect on the above. *Is* your current path helping you in your personal growth? *Are* you becoming more aware through its practice? Reiki Healing, at least when used in the way described in this book, has some important features:

* It emphasises and encourages self-responsibility. It enables us to take control of our own healing process.

* It connects us to the world around us and helps us to accept and live in 'the real world' . . . *all* aspects of it!

* It can easily become part of our day-to-day life, an integrated part of our being, not an isolated practice.

Many would point out that meditation, yoga, Alexander Technique, self hypnosis and other techniques can be used in the same way. They can, very successfully. It's not so much which technique or therapy you use but how you use it. When we are aware of what we're trying to achieve - to become more aware, to reconnect to our true self in the normal world - then any therapy can take on a more useful function in your life. As we become more aware so our awareness improves . . . once our conscious mind sees the benefits the process becomes automatic . . . we live to grow.

Reiki - Without Rules

Yes, But . . .

This idea of replacing rules from society and upbringing with Divine Order may sound very appealing . . . but it is not an easy option. Such freedom comes only through surrender of long held beliefs. And how can we be sure that we *are* truly listening to our higher self? Are we aware enough of our own thought processes to hear and act on our inner voice? Could we use all this as an excuse for just doing what we *want* to?

Yes, we could. But any such self deception will inevitably bring about a suitable chastisement . . . eventually. *Some years ago (pre Reiki) I had a bad cold and was taking conventional medication for it. I was feeling rough and should have stayed at home in bed. However I felt I had to drive to the nearby town to deliver something which had been hanging around for a while. I delivered the item OK, but whilst driving home mis-judged an on-coming car at a junction and ran into it. In hind-sight I was not fit to be driving. The urge to make the journey had been impatience. I suffered the consequences, of heightened insurance premiums and penalty points on the driving licence, for many years.*

So how can we tell if an urge to do something is our higher self or another, less whole, aspect of us? There may be no rules, but there are some useful pointers:

* Our inner voice, although sometimes insistent, will usually be calm. If we keep ignoring it, it might get persistent, but not angry. The inner voice speaks with love. By contrast our conditioning, bad habits, ego, etc. often *do* get angry. Their messages will have a sense of resentment, irritation and such feelings about them.

* Literally face ourselves or somebody else. When speaking the truth, we can look others in the eye. Truth can withstand eye contact, lies rarely can.

* Be aware of things happening around you. A 'chance' overheard comment or an article on TV might just confirm what your inner voice is trying to tell you.

* Our higher self is willing and able to face anything. Denial is a sign that our lower self is in charge - don't listen to it!

* When we start facing truths that part of us would rather not face, our bodies may well get in on the act.

I'd like to illustrate this last point with another pre-Reiki experience:

As a special treat, to help me prove to myself I could enjoy a holiday on my own, I'd booked 2 weeks in Barbados. A few nights before I was due to go I awoke with excruciating pains in my side. I tried all sorts of things but still they remained. I managed to get to the local GP as soon as the surgery opened - he told me to go straight to Casualty at the local hospital. The jabbing pains continued all morning. I was examined and tested . . . even had a ultra-sound scan, but the doctors could not discover what the problem was. I stayed in hospital a while under observation, but eventually the pain subsided and I went home. I went to Barbados and had a wonderful time. A year or two later, when faced with another new and significant challenge, I experienced similar pains. It dawned on me that these pains were basically fear . . . and the old me not wanting to move forward. I faced the fear, gradually managed to reassure myself that I was doing the right thing . . . and the pain went.

Now, whatever the symptom, I sense that my body is trying to tell me something. With Reiki I'm now able to tune into it, intuit what the real issue is . . . and deal with it. Pains may still persist, but only so long as I hold on to old ways.

Signs in Other

The above signs of truthful behaviour (or otherwise) are as true in others as they are in us . . . and often easier to spot.

Take denial, for example. From the outside it is easy to see that the more somebody denies a fact the more likely it is to be true . . . "I DON'T love him". "I'm over my mum's death", etc. Unfortunately, the more some-one is in denial, the less inclined they'll be to listen to the truth from others. Perhaps here we have a sign of a truly aware human being - someone who accepts that there might be truth in all things . . . and is prepared to consider unpleasant facts . . . even if they're personal and uncomplimentary.

For individuals not willing to face reality, we still have, and need, conventional rules, laws, and codes of conduct. We can have no freedom to do 'our thing' until we are mature enough to accept full responsibility for ourselves. Awareness is about seeing and accepting these realities of life.

Truth of the Matter

Perhaps awareness is about being able to recognise the truth - in all situations. Reiki has taught me that no truth can be written down or put into words. But writing CAN help bring things out from our mental closet . . . ALL thoughts, words, beliefs, etc. ARE stepping stones on our path to truth . . . no more, no less.

Thus I do not claim the ideas in this book to be truth. They represent, or at least have represented, various thoughts and feelings that I've had on my developmental path. A major lesson I'm being given however is in acceptance: learning to respect ALL views, all beliefs. There is a very good reason why each of us believes what we believe. I believe that the more open-minded we are, the more willing and able we are to rise beyond beliefs, the better. But that too is a belief! Who am I to claim this is a higher truth? And that really is my message here - *your* truth is *your* truth . . . and nobody else's. No other human (or channelled entity for that matter) can tell us what to think, do or believe . . . for we DO have free will! This spiritual journey we're on is about facing that aspect of ourselves, about seeing just how much choice we DO have!

Through the Reiki journey I've learnt (become aware) that I took many easy decisions in my youth. I chose not to face the competitive nature of life (by avoiding games at school). I chose not to face women when my grammar school turned comprehensive. But we can rarely ignore the lessons of life indefinitely. At some stage we have to face the consequences of our choices. Thus in recent years I've finally taken my blinkers off and chosen to face the realities of this world. With the help of Reiki I've been catching up with myself, getting back where I would have been had I faced reality as a youngster. That is not to berate myself. Part of the choice is to forgive our younger selves, to make peace with the us that *did* take the easy route. For eventually we find that there is no such thing as a free lunch. There is no easy path. The whole concepts of 'easy' and 'free' prevent us from moving forward. Labels such as these often cause the mental blocks that hold us back.

However, as we learn (through Reiki healing or similar techniques) to experience the mystic order to life, so we can put all this in perspective. Now the choices become clear: we can see out life as 'the journey home' and a quest for truth, or we can go along with the society around us. We can listen to the voice of the media and politicians . . . or to the still small voice of calm deep within us. THIS is our Free Will. Every moment we exercise it: Every time we choose to either let some fear govern our action or to face that fear; Every time we allow a habit to determine our action instead of listening to the guidance from our higher self.

This, it seems to me, is what becoming aware is all about. Recognising how our life is a result of our thoughts. Seeing things for what they are - at all levels.

When we choose to go along with our conditioned thoughts then we are choosing to keep the world we've inherited. When we chose to purify our thoughts, to life the Tao Way, or to take the Reiki Route (for example) then we are finally accepting our role in the world today . . . and taking our rightful place as spiritual beings. What that means to each of us is probably very different. There are no rules when we are truly exercising our free will . . . we each do what we *have* to do, what our soul requires us to do: *being* our true self.

Our divine nature has any answers we need, the Universe will provide for our needs. Our Will, the Will of God, the collective, universal, consciousness, is all embracing. We can choose to deny it, try to take our own route. Often we'll be allowed to . . . for that is how we learn! But the more we assert our independence from this One Life, the more likely will life show us the reality: There is no such thing as an accident. Watch any of the TV programmes centred around the emergency services and look at the victims in the lead up to their accident. Do we see a calm, centred, person, at peace with themselves and the world? Very, very rarely! More usually we'll see an individual who is, or feels themselves to be, isolated from everything and everybody else. We'll see denial, we'll see the whole range of emotions, expressed in the extreme. Talk about an accident waiting to happen! This could be any of us . . . if we ignore the warnings. If we keep asserting that our mental view of the world is reality. Our inner self knows the truth. When we choose to listen, we see how the chaos around us is of our own making . . . the Universe giving us the lessons we need to help us stop and look at things from a higher perspective.

In saying all that I'll probably be accused of judging those who've had impossible backgrounds. It is not my intent to label or to judge, merely to provide an alternative view of things. By denying it you may well be proving the point! The suggestion is also that just as we choose the life around us, by following our ego voice or soul voice, so we chose the life we came into when we entered this particular mind/body.

Somehow this theory is harder to swallow. It presupposes re-incarnation. Or does it? Not necessarily! It suggests that, at the soul/spirit level we each have a specific lesson to learn in this life - a soul purpose. This idea has been with us for some time and has been made popular, for example, by James Redfield in "The Celestine Prophecy" and "The Tenth Insight". If we need to learn about our inner (spiritual) strength, then perhaps we choose a particularly harsh life so that we get sufficient challenge to bring out that inner strength? If we need to learn how to take, about humility, perhaps we choose a life with MS (or similar disabling condition) so that we have no choice but to let others do things for us.

All of this *could* be explained in terms of Karma and 'making amends' for 'wrongs' in previous life. However, whether we see harsh lives as resulting from previous lives or a soul choice, some things don't change - the situation itself! i.e. does it really matter how or why we find ourselves in hard times? What matters is how we respond to the situation. If we insist on blaming others, or a previous life, then we'll retain the 'victim' tag and with it, in all probability, a feeling of dissatisfaction with life.

If, on the other hand, we accept that this is the way it is and seek to learn what we can from the experience, *then* we'll find some sort of fulfilment and meaning to our life. At times, knowing 'why' can help us move forward. There probably *is* a reason for all things - if we look deep enough. Identifying our soul purpose can help along this track.

Thus, ideas such as soul purpose fit nicely onto the Reiki Route. Once committed to finding our true self, then to have a sense as to what we are and why we came here can help us to bring focus (and thus meaning) to our lives. But don't let it take you over! Again, it's just a model, just a way of giving our conscious mind some explanation as to why things are the way they are . . . so that we can move forward.

OK, so lets put this in practice!

Underlying Cause

What is annoying you most here and now? As you read this, who or what makes you feel angry or irritated or resentful? Picture the situation and sense it in sights, sounds, feelings. Any way it feels most real to you. Allow the feelings to surface and express them - cry, laugh, scream - whatever is necessary. Let the initial emotions come and go. Then ask yourself what it is that you're REALLY angry/sad (or whatever) about. Perhaps you feel that somebody is behaving selfishly, for example. Now ask yourself "am I behaving selfishly". Be honest with yourself. Often what we accuse others of is true of ourselves. They are merely mirrors of our own behaviour! The cause of our dis-ease or dis-stress is that we are not being true to ourselves . . . and we know it! Our Soul knows the truth. The Universe knows the truth. When we genuinely seek to understand and accept the realities of our lives, they'll be presented to us! Reiki connects us to the truth and helps us to accept it.

Reiki - Without Rules

36 - Back to where we started

Life is characterised by cycles. Everything seems to come round again sooner or later. Many find as they tread the path of Reiki (or similar) that they're taken back to their childhood or reconnected to old friends. There is no escape from the past. If we are to be free to live each moment fully we have to be at peace with all that's come before. It somehow seems appropriate that I get a distinct feeling of Deja Vu as I write this!

Another characteristic of the learning process called life is that each lesson seems to come not as something new, but as a memory. The truth, when it hits us, isn't new but something we've always known but had forgotten. Thus any path of enlightenment is about dusting off these truths, returning to the simplicity and purity that we once knew. Whether we knew them as infants or as incarnating spirits is a matter of debate . . . it probably doesn't matter. Such thoughts would not have occurred to us in either case.

Many start their spiritual journey through feeling lost in their lives. *Knowing* that there is something more. Tired of so much of what our current civilisation considered important. Some will even describe themselves as aliens - beings from the Pleiades or the Sirius System. They put their feelings of alienation from earth society down to the fact that they *are* beings from a different world. And who can blame them. So much in conventional society disconnects us from our spiritual selves. It is often near impossible to listen to our inner voice above the marketing hype and noise of today. But we chose to come here. This life is of our making. Likewise, we can change it. Through what we do (and don't do), what we say (and don't say) and through what we think (or don't think) we *can* bring about a life in which we feel more fulfilled, more real. This is where

Reiki as a way of life brings us and takes us. Reiki Healing is a tool to help us dig ourselves out of the rut. Healing makes us whole. It brings us Home. I look forward to meeting you there!

Nothing Means Anything

The great Freddie Mercury of the group Queen provided us with an excellent affirmation on our path:

> *Nothing Really Matters*
> *Anyone can see*
> *Nothing Really Matters to Me*

After singing this at times of frustration, over a number of years, gradually my logical mind accepted the idea. *Nothing* matters so much that we need get worked up and upset by it. As is emphasised a number of times in this book, emotional detachment from the world around is a useful aim on the path to enlightenment. Reiki, in taking us to a place where not just our senses but our very soul, tingles, helps the process in many ways.

But it's not just being free of emotions that constitutes true freedom. It is perhaps about being free of *all* thoughts . . . free of all constructions of the conscious mind.

Until we become aware of just how active our thoughts are, it's hard to appreciate just what this means. But with Reiki, and it's partners on the path, we become conscious of the energy we waste in unproductive reasoning. And so we slowly discard our ego activity.

'Nothing means anything' because 'meaning' is an activity of the conscious mind, an attempt to define the undefinable, to control that which is beyond the capacity of humans to control . . . life itself. Take anything which we might, at some time in our life, have considered important, meaningful, and look at it in the light of pure love and truth - it evaporates, it dissolves, as everything does, into the light itself. It has no meaning, no real significance, save that we attach to it.

Thus, as we apply our Reiki symbols at the things (or rather ideas) that bother us, so they each in turn loose their significance. Gradually we see that even the state of our bank balance or the presence (or otherwise) of a significant other in our lives are just irrelevant thoughts. Meaningless in the cosmic scheme of things.

But . . . Yes? But what? A life without emotions? A life without thoughts? Sounds dull and boring, devoid of all that makes life, life? Only because we're afraid of that void . . . and what can come from and through it! Only because we're afraid to let go of these brain activities that we've become so used to. The brain/mind works far better when we free it of unnecessary activity . . . just as a computer works far better when we exit all programmes we don't actually need and purge old files from memory.

Being free of thoughts and emotions doesn't mean no feelings! On the contrary. Without all the conditioned reactions we're free - in mind and body - to truly sense and feel the here and now. To enter into the moment with *all* of us present . . . mind, body and soul. As we do so, life becomes a joy. This is happiness! This is living.

Whilst writing this piece I felt nauseous. Not an emotional nervousness, but a sense of fear caused by an idea I didn't want to stomach. The old controlling me not wanting to surrender. I put my hands on my stomach and treat the sensation. Within a few minutes the sense of feeling sick had gone. Another fear conquered. The result - a greater range of situations faced without that fear . . . a greater freedom to enjoy life.

From nothing . . . to nothing

So, what's life all about? We search for some meaning only to find that, if anything, it's the search itself that matters most. We desire to 'come home' only to find that home is probably where we started from - a sense of being, a One-ness, where our 'self' (whatever that means) is totally immersed in love and part of it. On the spiritual path we put aside the notion that material wealth, power, fame (and the like) are really, of themselves, worthwhile aims.

And then we have the idea that 'what goes around comes around', or 'as ye reap, so shall ye mow'. Philosophy and experience tend to agree that what we say and do in our lives will come back to bless or haunt us, eventually. Again the circle.

The circle of many philosophies - the serpent eating its own tail. No end. Always life brings us right back where we started. We could argue that it's a spiral rather than a circle, in that there will be *some* change the next time around, but only as part of a greater circle. A circle within a circle. Life's great cycle. There's no escaping it. To attempt to do so is suicide - for our true, spiritual, self. We are subject to the laws of the Universe - not those defined by scientists, but the Divine Law, the Mystic Order. Within that order we have a purpose, life is real.

To the human mind conditioned to be in control, this all sounds rather fatalistic. It can be a depressing thought that we're just going to end up where we started. But is it? On the contrary! If we, at some level, know where we're heading, then what is there is to worked up about? If the Universe is looking after us and has all our needs under its omnipotence, then why don't we just relax and enjoy life?

It's all summed up by Eric Idle (of Monty Python fame) in the song he recorded (in the late 80's) "Always look on the bright side of life". Within it he says

"You've come from nothing, you're going back to nothing. What have you lost? Nothing!"

Man's intellectual phase has been about learning to see our place in the cosmic order of things. It's been necessary - to reason things out, to create and develop models of life as we know it. But the time is coming when we are ready to accept that we *are* just one species of being amongst many. Reiki and its like are helping us to face this reality. That is its purpose.

Research into NDE (Near Death Experiences) shows that as we approach death we are shown the results of our thoughts, words and deeds. We are given the experience of feeling what it was like to be on the receiving end of our own temper . . . our love, our own hate . . our consideration. The message is clear - what we receive in life *is* a mirror of what we give out.

The philosophy 'do as you would be done by' is particularly relevant to Reiki teachers. If we teach restrictive practices and dogmas, then by those same dogmas we'll be bound. If, on the other hand, we encourage openness and teach the channelling of love under any name, then we'll be rewarded with love from all directions.

We are ready now to surrender as 'all conquering' mankind and take our place as true, whole, human beings. As such we can fully interact and interrelate to all cultures, all other life-forms, all other beings. It is this full interaction - living in mind, body and soul, that will give us a sense of fulfilment little known to our intellectual selves. It's our inheritance . . . where we came from! Reiki is taking us, bringing us, home.

Reiki and Soul Mates

You may well find that as you take up Reiki you'll meet up with people with whom you feel a particular affinity. Sometimes it will be obvious what this is (a mutual interest in previous lives and/or being from the Pleiades for example) at other times, it won't. But there will be an energy between you. One way of explaining this (and it's only a possible model) is that this other person and you have a soul connection. Perhaps you made a pact, before you came here, to help each other in a particular way. Or perhaps you're from the same 'soul family' - you have the same fundamental aspect of spiritual energy, 'gentle souls' for example.

Another way of explaining such a powerful sense of being connected to somebody, is a 'resonance of need'. i.e. your mind/body is radiating your particular needs and when it meets somebody that can satisfy those needs, we'll feel this attractive force. When the needs of *both* individuals can be met by a 'coming together', then the energy resonates - it builds up into tangible feelings . . . to help us recognise that this is a situation we need to act on.

This sort of thing happens anyway, but as Reiki people we'll tend to be more aware of it. And, being 'better connected' ourselves, so our own energies will be more powerful. We'll be clearer (at least subconsciously) about our particular needs. Quite literally we'll be sending out signals to attract to us that which we need.

The emphasis here is on 'need'. That which will assist our soul purpose. Often not the same thing as 'want'! Thus we may find ourselves drawn to a member of the opposite sex and want a relationship with them. Not a good idea to fall in love with them when the mutual need is for someone to sing with or dance with . . . and no more! Sometimes the need will be to be tempted, to help us see the deeper reality of such attractions. This certainly happened to me on a few occasions! I sense this connection, what I perceived as a mutual need, only to find that other factors in the situations were not 'right' for us to come together at all! Or maybe the need is for a night of intimacy, but no more . . . or to allow a contact to be established with a mutual friend. There are no rules with Soul Mates. Each connection we sense has a particular meaning and need associated with it - some will be over in seconds, some may last (at least) the rest of this lifetime.

So how do we find out the significance of a given attraction? We need to see things in perspective, to see not just the aspect that drew us together but other factors. An ideal job for Reiki:

Perspective

Bring to mind the person for whom you feel an affinity. See their face in your mind's eye. If it appears to one side of the mind, try to shift it centrally - it may be just a dream! [See 'Of One Mind' in Chapter 33]

Now 'take yourself off' - perhaps see yourself floating out of your window and rising into the sky, up, up until the earth is a dot. Take in the beauty of the scene and the wonder of creation. Look around, is your soul friend still with you? If not, maybe the connection isn't as strong as you thought.

If they are, then acknowledge them. Take their hand and fly together in the sky. Does this feel 'right', does this feel good? With a true soul friend, the sense of oneness with the cosmos will probably be increased by joining together. Or perhaps they seem to pull you down to earth? Look at them. Is there something pulling THEM down? An earthly attachment? A partner?

Look around, listen and sense. Ask for the truth and allow it to be shown to you. Perhaps another person comes into view, or a particular place. Bring yourself back down into where you are sitting or lying. Is the person still with you? In what circumstance? If the two of you are inseparable in a ball of bliss, then this IS a soul-mate! If not, see the reality. KNOW that this was just a temptation, or a brief encounter . . . or is a friendship of a kindred spirit. Look and listen. The limits (if any!) to the connection will be shown to you. Know this, and you could save yourself (and them) much heartache.

Nothing Wasted

We all do our best, all the time. The concepts of mistakes, errors, etc. are the result of a human mind intent on controlling things. In reality all we do by labelling something a mistake is to do ourselves down. By saying we've done something wrong, all we're doing is knocking our own self confidence - not a good idea.

Maybe, in making a particular decision, we make things more difficult than they need have been. However once that decision is taken it will take us through experiences from which we will certainly benefit. Everything we do is a lesson from which we learn. No opportunity is wasted to explore ourselves and the world around us. And, when we see life in this light, we can see a positive side to all situations.

Likewise, all the skills and lessons we've learnt in the past will prove to be of benefit as we consciously commit to our spiritual journey. On the face of it, I changed tracks completely by moving from Quality Assurance (QA) in the Electronics industry to teaching Reiki. But on closer inspection, all of my experiences working on the reliability of silicon chips (and such things) is proving invaluable in this current role:

* As a QA man I was always looking for the best and how to achieve it. Then it was in a piece of state-of-the art technology, now it is in people.

* In the electronics industry I was dealing with flows of electrons and electro-magnetic radiation, now I'm dealing with other subtle energies.

* My role as 'catalyst and lubricant' started in my early days of employment and hasn't ever really stopped.

The Universe knows what lessons we need, knows what we're here to learn and to achieve and guides us into the jobs and relationships we most need to experience.

So, if you're unsure of your direction in life, look at what you've already done. Not in conventional terms, but in terms of lessons and skills learnt. Identify what it's been that has made you feel most 'you' and allow that part of you to suggest your next move. Remember that our most important 'work' is that which helps our soul on its journey home. One student of mine for example had for many years been working in the fraud office of a major service company: her search for the truth then providing a wonderful basis for her wider search for truth through Reiki!

Above and Beyond

Whatever religious, philosophical or other path takes us there, once we have experienced that sense of One-ness, then divisions disappear. Words, we then know, are but feeble attempts to convey the indescribable. Once we *know* that all paths lead to this reunion between our mind-body and our true, divine, self, then theories, beliefs and models loose their attraction. We are better off without them. For specific beliefs, and adherence to them, limit our way of thinking. Specific theories, and development of them, take us away from the *experience* of oneness . . . and that is where we are heading . . . ask anyone who's been 'there'!

All the things that we do through Reiki, we do not just for ourselves, but for life itself. Reiki, the flow of love, is a sharing. The Universe really appreciates all the love we give. Our friends in higher realms (angels, spirit guides, beings from other galaxies) *do* welcome our commitment to our path. They know how difficult it is for us to leave behind the old humans ways. The thanks they give us when we *do* open our hearts and minds to them can be profound: A wonderful sense of gratitude. By being true to our real selves, by living in the light, so we are doing our bit to bring 'heaven to earth', for want of a better phrase. But not just to earth. The efforts we make, our choices, our love, sends ripples throughout the Universe. Our mind:body may be on an earthly journey but our soul is on a cosmic one, an integral part of the evolution of creation. It is said by some that the efforts taken towards enlightenment by so many humans has already helped to prevent a major catastrophe for our planet. As those on a spiritual journey live more and more openly and as part of society, so this becomes the predominant way for men and women to live. We *are* bringing about a new sort of society . . . and probably also helping our friends in others realms and worlds forward on *their* paths.

In passing

So why write a book? *Because I had to!* Because it has been part of my purpose and journey. Only by writing down my thoughts and theories have I been able to clarify in my own mind that none of them really matter. It is my hope that by presenting alternative ideas, those on a spiritual path are encouraged to 'let go' of limited and limiting beliefs. By sharing a freer, more open, view of life, hopefully we will all move that bit closer to a world that places divine wisdom above 'proven' fact and 'right action' above doing what we *should* do.

It is true that scientific theories, philosophical models and other ideas have helped us move from animals to thinking beings, but our next phase of human evolution integrates our mind, body and soul, it sees us live as One. The role of words and beliefs, be they in religion, science or any other facet of life, is now to help it come together. The big breakthroughs are coming through Interdisciplinary work - Chaos theory is relevant to all scientists, biologists, physicists, cosmologists, etc. and by working together they'll all see the One-ness that is life. This spreads within and between all of their disciplines.

Likewise the church work that gains most praise and support these days is that that 'brings together': Interfaith celebrations, Inter-denominational worships, churches working in, for and with communities to regenerate true community spirit. Religious groups working *with* artists and musicians from all cultures. God, by whatever name we call him, her or it, *is* within *all* of us. Reiki is but one path to our immersion in a soul-centred human world.

Another path I've found maybe as useful as Reiki . . . and which I've used alongside it, is writing: particularly penning poems to express my non-establishment views. The following, for example, helped me break free of conventional rigid grammatical rules in my writing:

BEYOND BELIEF

Is there a God of Grammar?
Maybe
For even the studious are blessed

But . .

Beyond Belief we fly with angels
Without Words we soar through heaven
Free of expectations we truly live

Sentences surrender to serenity
Paragraphs pass away into eternity

So lets Dot The I that is 1
Cross the T we drink at 3
And Question the mark that humanity has left on creation

Let us sentence ourselves no more
Let us write, and live
As our souls dictate

Reiki - Without Rules

Whole Reiki

In this book we've explored 'Reiki in the World', how this system of healing can help us live a more natural, true, life. I hope that I've been able to remove some of the restrictions and limiting beliefs that are often presented with The Usui System. Reiki, the energy, is within us all. Thus its use, as part of our personal growth, can have no limitations . . . save those we impose on ourselves in our own minds.

To get the best from Reiki healing we need to see it in the broadest picture . . . it is, after all, an holistic therapy! In this book, we've looked at how Reiki relates to many specific aspects of our life . . . and to life in general:

* Our Mind. Reiki helps us to see that most, if not all, of our dis-ease and distress results from the way we think and what's become locked in our heads. Reiki gives us a way of working directly on such mental blocks. Hopefully the explanations given in this book also help our rational mind to understand and accept what's happening to us as we tread the Reiki Route.

* Our Body. Our inner self uses our body to talk to us. All the answers to our 'problems' lie within us. Reiki healing helps us to tune into the source of wisdom and thus to relax us physically.

* Our Soul. For our sake and the sake of humanity, it's time we all accepted that we are spiritual beings. Reiki reconnects us to our spiritual self. It brings our minds and bodies back into alignment with our soul and its purpose here.

* The World Around. The environment and society around us are mirrors of our minds. As we face our truths, so we see the realities of mankind . . . and vice versa. Reiki helps us to see that we are One. Everything is interconnected. We cannot escape the realities of life, but with Reiki we have a tool to help us face it and enjoy it again.

* The Universe. Quite often (always?) any sense of frustration in life comes when we fail to acknowledge the wonder, wisdom and power

of the universe. Reiki reconnects us. Reiki IS this wonder, wisdom and power . . . *and* it is US! We are of, in and part of this amazing, multidimensional, cosmic, divine, creation. But really, it's beyond words. It just IS . . . and Reiki helps us to see and feel this.

So, forget all that you've read here or in any other book on Reiki. Reiki just IS . . . or at least, it's what YOU need it to be . . . here and now. Reiki, the energy and the system of healing, helps you to be YOU. The real you.

Postscript

Most of this book was first written in the late nineteen nineties and early twenty noughties (!) . . . as I became aware of a higher truth in and through my practice and teaching of Reiki. At the time however getting the book published just didn't happen. The time was not right. Now, around Easter 2007, I KNOW I have to get these words of mine out into the world . . . for them to do whatever they need to.

Why the delay and why now? Reasons don't really matter any more, not when one follows a higher guidance, but

* the Easter period is always a good one to move forward with new truths.

* as I wrote this book, my ideas were just that. Deeply felt opinions, but I have to admit, merely theories. In the intervening years, as I lived these ideas and learnt many more practical lessons in their day-to-day applications, so I can be far more sure of their truth, relevance and significance.

* by way of further reassurance on the above point, a number of other books and authors are saying very similar things, about our need to let go of our personal history, our ego control and 'Flat-land' thinking. This year I've read and been inspired by: Paulo Coelho's "The Zahir", Eckhart Tolle's "A New Earth" and Ken Wilbur's "A Brief History of Everything". Coming from very different places and writing in very different ways, the message of new direction . . . and of hope, is clear in them all.

* just talking to other people, whether consciously on a path or not, and reading reports from other light workers all illustrate just how many of us ARE 'on a journey'.

May your journey be joyous, may this book help you accept. My blessings to you.

Index of Key Words

To make this more useful to you as a reference book we include an index of the topics (as relevant to Reiki) that are covered. The page number given is one of the primary reference - there may be others.

References

Every book has something to offer somebody. It's usually the ones that you're given or that (literally) fall off the shelf at you that you need at any given moment. The following is a list (in no particular order) of some of the books that have helped me on my path:

Bodo Baginski & Shalila Sharamon "Reiki Universal Life Energy - Self-treatment and the Home Professional Practice"; Life Rhythm Publication; ISBN 0-940795-02-7

Paula Horan "Empowerment through Reiki - The path to personal and global transformation"; Lotus Light, Shangri-La Series; ISBN 0-941524-84-1

Frank Arjava Petter "Reiki Fire"; Lotus Light, Shangri-La Series; ISBN 0-914955-50-0

Diane Stein "Essential Reiki - A complete guide to an ancient healing art"; The Crossing Press; ISBN 0-89594-736-6

Serena Roney-Dougal "Where Science & Magic meet"; Element Books; ISBN 1-85230-446-4

Fritjof Capra "Belonging to the Universe - New Thinking about God and Nature"; Penguin; ISBN 0-14-017239-4

Murry Hope "Time - the Ultimate Energy"; Element; ISBN 1-85230-237-2

Doreen Virtue "Goddess Guidance Oracle Cards" and many others

James Gleick "Chaos - Making a New Science"; Penguin

James Gleick (with photos by Eliot Porter) "Nature's Chaos"; Cardinal: ISBN 0-7474-0759-2

Paramhansa Yogananda " The Autobiography of a Yogi"

Richard Bach "There's No Such Place As Far Away", "Illusions", "One", "Bridge Across Forever"

Paulo Coelho - "The Alchemist", "The Zahir", etc.

David Abram "The Spell of the Sensuous"; Vintage Books; ISBN 0-679-77639-7

Julie Soskin "The Wind of Change"; Ashgrove Press; ISBN 1-85398-075-7

Betty Shine "Mind Magic", "My Life as a Medium", etc.

James Redfield "The Celestine Prophecy" & "The Tenth Insight"

Mother Meera "Answers"; Rider; ISBN 0-7126-5372-4

Diana Cooper "a little light on Ascension"; Findhorn Press; ISBN 1-899171-81-9 (and others)

Aldous Huxley "The Doors of Perception/Heaven & Hell"; Harper Collins (Flamingo); ISBN 0-00-654731-1

Stephen Batchelor "Buddhism without Beliefs - A contemporary guide to awakening"; Bloomsbury; ISBN 0-7475-3769-0

Clive Barker "Imajica", Harper Collins; ISBN 0-00-223559-5

Barry & Joyce Vissell "The Shared Heart - Relationship Initiations & Celebrations"; Ramira Publishing; ISBN 0-9612720-0-7

Robert Bly "Iron John - A book about men"; Element; ISBN 1-85230-233-X

Phyllis V Schlemmer & Palden Jenkins (compilers) "The Only Planet of Choice"; Gateway Books; ISBN 1-85860-004-9

David Knight "Pathway. The Channelled Love & Wisdom from the transleations of the two sisters star group"; DPK Publishing; ISBN 0-9532824-0-6

Beatrice Russell "Beyond the Veils - Through Meditation"; Lincoln Philosophical Research Foundation;

Michel Desmarquet "Thiaooba Prophecy"; Arafura Publishing; ISBN 0-646-31395-9

Ken Wilbur "A Brief History of Everything"; ISBN 0-7171-3233-1

Contacts

UK Reiki Federation,
PO Box 1785,
Andover
SP11 OWB
UK
enquiry@reikifed.co.uk
www.reikifed.co.uk/

Scientific & Medical Network
www.scimednet.org/

New Games
www.inewgames.com

Positive News
No5 Bicton Enterprise Centre
Clun
Shropshire
SY7 8NF
UK
office@positivenews.org.uk
www.positivenews.org.uk

A Reiki meditation

Does your mind wonder whilst doing your Reiki self-treatment? If you would you like something to focus on mentally whilst doing Reiki, then this meditation may well help. It is designed to accompany any Reiki session and is based on the Louise Hay's *Heal Your Body* - i.e. the correlation between each part of our bodies (and it's associated ailments) and our mental attitudes, beliefs, etc..

The following can be used as a basis for your own statements, affirmations and reflection on how we create our health and life situations through what and how we think. By doing this DURING a Reiki treatment we'll further emphasis our intent to tune into our own highest good, release old thought patterns (and associated diseases, ill-health, etc) and realign mind and body to our soul purpose and natural divine state.

Also interwoven into this meditation are the Reiki Principles, so adding a further level of commitment to the Reiki path to self improvement.

EYES

I thank the universe for my ability to see. I ask that I be better able to see the truth, and only the truth, as I look around me in the world. Help me to see and accept those things that I've previously denied or not liked about myself, about others or about life. Help me to see the best in others that I may compliment and encourage them.

THIRD-EYE, FOREHEAD

I thank the universe for my sixth sense, my intuition and my ability to see beyond our 3-Dimensional world. Help me to trust this highest of senses. Help me to tune into those I share my part of this planet with, be they human, animal or whatever, to understand, accept and respect their part in our one interconnected life.

CHIN

I thank the universe for my teeth, mouth and jaws . . . and for my ability to eat all the wonderful food that nature provides for us. Help me to eat that which bests serves my body and soul at this time. Help me also to be able to swallow unpalatable facts and to take-in the truth that I may love and accept life as it really is.

BACK OF HEAD

I thank the universe for my mind, by ability to think, to remember. Help me however to accept that my conscious mind is nothing compared to the collective consciousness and the wisdom of the one-ness. Help me to find peace of mind, to accept myself, to feel safe as the unique human being that I am. Help me to find harmony between my mind, body and soul.

SHOULDERS

I thank the universe for my shoulders, for my arms and hands and my ability to carry, hold and grasp. Help me also to grasp the underlying and higher truth in difficult situations. Help me to shoulder my responsibility for my life, my health and to offer up all other perceived responsibilities to the angels.

HEART, RIBS, CHEST

I thank the universe for the amazing things that are my heart and lungs and their ability to keep me supplied with the vital breath of life. Help me to be open in my receipt of fresh air . . . and love. Help me to love and respect others (of whatever species) unconditionally.

STOMACH & ABDOMEN

I thank the universe for my ability to digest food that I may be filled with energy by which to live. Help me to also to digest fear, to stomach uncertainty and to be at peace with my emotions.

HIPS

I thank the universe for my hips and legs that carry me wherever I go. Help me to move forward in my life with joy and balance.

KNEES

I thank the universe for my knees and joints and for the flexibility they allow in my movements. Help me to be flexible too in my decisions, help me to surrender my ego to the greater good and to kneel with humility.

FEET

I thank the universe for my ankles and feet and the ability to walk, run, climb, etc. Help me to walk humbly and with divine authority, to know when to stride forward purposefully and when to retreat gracefully. Help me to be able to change direction when necessary and to know when I'm on the path that's right for me.

BACK OF NECK

I thank the universe for my neck and the ability to rotate my head in SO many ways! Help me to look around me, to be aware of what's behind and to the side of me. Help me to look up and look down and to change my perspective on life and situations that I may be at peace with myself and others.

SHOULDER BLADES

I thank the universe for my shoulder blades, my upper and middle back that support my body as I move through life. Help me to be aware of the emotional support that is always available to me from the angels.

SMALL OF BACK, KIDNEYS

I thank the universe for my lower back and its physical support to my whole body . . . and for my kidneys for eliminating the waste.

Help me also to eliminate my negative thoughts and old emotions that I may grow up to be(come) the whole and real me.

COCYX

I thank the universe for the vital and flexible support of my skeleton, for the seat of by being. Help me to get to the bottom of any distress or dis-ease and to know that I am safe and secure at all times.

Other books by the author

During his personal journey, Keith has used writing as a major part of his facing of himself and the truth. Now settled in the Algarve and living a life more in tune with his higher needs, he's gradually working on his 'growth writing' from his years of new awakenings and publishing those books that will hopefully be of help and support to other. For a list of current titles, visit www.pintados.co.uk (Keith & Liz's site) or www.lulu.com/k13 (Keith's listing on his publisher's site).

At the time of writing *Reiki - Without Rules*, Keith's other published books are:

* *A Brave New World Emerging* (ISBN: 978-1-84753-034-9) is a collection of poems from the heart. Sharing Keith's person quest for truth and identity, they also encourage anyone to put their own thoughts and feeling into verse.

* *Rosy Tinted Glasses* (ISBN: 978-1-84753-246-6) is truly unique. Containing images by Northants artist Julie Rose Bills, it provides a series of powerful guided meditations which will not only relax you but inspire a deep connection to your imagination and all the insights that that brings with it.